Stumpwork
Seasons

Dedication

To Neva and Pam

Stumpwork Seasons

Kay & Michael Dennis

SEARCH PRESS

First published in Great Britain 2007

Search Press Limited
Wellwood, North Farm Road,
Tunbridge Wells, Kent TN2 3DR

Reprinted 2008

Text copyright © Kay Dennis and Michael Dennis 2007

Website: www.kaydennis.co.uk

Photographs by Charlotte de la Bédoyère, Search Press Studios;
and Roddy Paine Photographic Studio
Photographs and design copyright © Search Press Ltd.

ISBN: 978-1-84448-041-8

Suppliers
If you have difficulty in obtaining any of the materials and
equipment mentioned in this book, please visit the Search Press
website for details of suppliers:
www.searchpress.com

Alternatively, you can visit the authors' website:
www.kaydennis.co.uk
to obtain materials and equipment, including a full-sized copy of
the template, via their own mail-order service.

Printed in Malaysia

Publishers' note
All the step-by-step photographs in this book feature
the authors, Kay and Michael Dennis, demonstrating
stumpwork techniques. No models have been used.

Acknowledgements

*To all our friends and students who continue to
support and encourage us. To Patricia Wood of
Mulberry Silks, Wendy James of Mace & Nairn, and
Jean Oliver of Oliver Twists.*

*Special thanks must go to Lotti and Roz at Search
Press, and especially our Editor, Katie, who has shown
unending patience as we constantly change our minds
about the content of the embroidery.*

*We would not have been able to write this book
without those people who taught Kay embroidery,
needlelace and stumpwork. Thanks go to Cathy Barley,
Pat Gibson, Doreen Holmes and Denise Montgomery,
with special thanks to Roy and Barbara Hirst.*

*This book is in recognition of all our students who
constantly present us with new challenges – challenges
that fuel our inspiration and enthusiasm for
discovering new and exciting initiatives in stumpwork.*

Contents

Introduction

The concept of producing an embroidery illustrating the four seasons was originally conceived during discussions at one of Kay's sewing days. One of the ladies present, Neva, sketched out a large circle with pictures showing the four seasons arranged around it; this sketch eventually formed the basis of two books: *Stumpwork Figures*, which was published by Search Press in 2006, and this book, *Stumpwork Seasons*.

Although the original design has evolved considerably, the basic idea is still the same: four pictures, depicting the four seasons, are arranged in a circle, each merging into the next to represent the constant, seamless changing of the seasons throughout the year. The design is based loosely on that of traditional seventeenth-century stumpwork embroideries, in which the various elements were often the same size, so a flower, for example, could be as large as a tree or an animal. As much of the space as possible was filled, and elaborately embroidered, larger-than-life insects were often used to fill in any gaps.

Although the embroidery is designed as a single piece, we have structured the book so that it is possible to produce four separate embroideries, each depicting a different season, and we have included clear instructions for all the stitches and techniques used. We hope that by doing this, those of you who are relatively new to the art of stumpwork will be able to gain as much enjoyment and satisfaction from this book as the more accomplished embroiderer.

The finished embroidery, just over half actual size.

The first stage in the development of the design was to list everything we wanted to include in each season. We then decided on the background colours. Symmetry and balance are provided by the blue water at the bottom of the picture and the blue winter's sky and snow at the top; and by the greens and browns of spring and autumn on either side. The two trees provide stability and strength, as well as framing the whole picture. Water plays an important part in the overall design; it forms the main component of the summer scene, and blends in to the centre of the picture, drawing everything together. The rocks and grass at the water's edge provide the boundaries between summer, spring and autumn, and the wall and fence form the outer limits of winter.

Once the background elements were in place, we reconsidered what we wanted to include in each season. We decided to put in as many elements as we could without overcrowding, and to use a broad range of colours, textures and techniques, achieving, we hoped, the richness and diversity that typified traditional stumpwork embroideries.

Materials and equipment

All the materials used in stumpwork are generally available from good needlework shops. Mail-order outlets, which advertise in needlework magazines, and the internet are also good sources of materials.

Threads

A very wide range of threads can be used in stumpwork – cotton, silk, metallic, synthetic and wool, all in hundreds of different colours and textures, and each creating a different result. With experience, you will learn how to select the correct thread for the effect you want to achieve. Fine threads work best in stumpwork, for example 100/3 silks or one strand of six-stranded cotton. We like using space-dyed threads to create interesting finishes, preferring hand-dyed to machine-dyed ones as the latter can produce a less attractive, stripey effect. Always use the best threads you can afford; some of the cheaper stranded cottons shred and fluff easily, giving an untidy appearance to your embroidery.

We have used mainly **stranded cottons**, **stranded silks** and **100/3 silk threads** in this book; silks give a lovely sheen to the stitches and are especially good for flowers and insects. The only other threads we have used are a **bouclé wool**, **fine tapestry wool** and **metallic thread**. A tubular metallic thread known as **bullion** has been used for the dragonfly's body. We use **sewing cotton** for work that is not going to be visible on the finished embroidery, for example for securing pads and couching down the cordonnet threads.

Needles & pins

Always use a needle that is appropriate for the purpose. It should pass through the fabric easily, and it should have an eye large enough to take the thread you are using comfortably, but not so big that the thread keeps falling out. We regularly use the following types of needle for stumpwork: **embroidery needles** are used for all embroidery stitches where the threads pass through the fabric. They have long eyes and sharp points. **Sharps needles** are good for all general sewing. We use **ballpoint needles** for making needlelace and for surface stitching, and a **darning needle** to help pass wires through the background fabrics.

We use **lace pins**, which are similar to dressmaker's pins but with a longer and thinner shank, for holding small pieces of needlelace in position before sewing them in place. **Berry-head** and **flower-head pins** are used for securing larger pieces of embroidery.

Kay's pincushion, showing the range of needles and pins she uses.

Basic sewing equipment

A **thimble** is especially useful when sewing through leather and other tough materials. **Tweezers** are used for handling very small pieces of embroidery such as needlelace and slips, and for removing small trimmings of thread. A **crochet hook** is used in needlelace to help lay the cordonnet. Always use sharp **scissors** – a large pair for cutting fabrics, a general-purpose pair for cutting paper, wire, etc., and a small, very sharp-pointed pair for cutting threads. It is advisable to buy the best you can afford; a good pair of scissors are an embroiderer's best friend and, if well cared for, will last a long time.

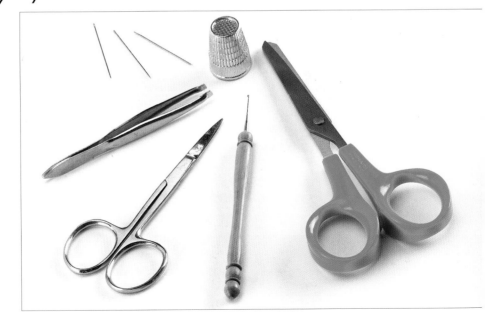

Background fabrics

Two layers of a plain background fabric, strong enough to support the sometimes heavily padded and wired elements, should be used for stumpwork. We have used a lightweight **calico** as the background fabric for this project, with a layer of medium-weight calico underneath. Lightweight calico was also used to make the slips for the sheep, the deer and the stag, the squirrel's body and autumn tree.

The ferns and the squirrel's tail have been embroidered on to **silk organza**. Because it is very sheer, the embroidered elements can be cut out, and any surplus fabric will not be visible against the calico background.

Silk chiffon is a soft, floaty fabric which has been used as the top layer on the water; when painted it gives a rippled effect. Unpainted chiffon placed over a painted background will give it a misty appearance. To give a rough texture to the grassy area at the base of the picture, we have used **silk noil**. The freestanding daffodil petals have been embroidered on to **watersoluble fabric**. It is tough enough for hand embroidery, but can be dissolved away from the stitching, which can then be sewn on to the background fabric.

Frames

Mounting the background fabrics in a frame will help keep a good tension on your work. **Circular embroidery frames** or **hoops** are available in many sizes and are very easy to use. The background fabric is supported between two concentric rings, the outer one of which can be adjusted using a screw clamp. **Silk frames** and pins are used for stretching fabric before it is painted.

Tip

Binding the inner ring of an embroidery hoop will help keep the fabric taut. Use strips of cotton sheeting cut on the bias.

Other fabrics and materials

Polyester toy stuffing has been used to fill three-dimensional elements. It pulls out to almost single strands and can be pushed into the smallest of spaces. Quilters' wadding is not suitable for stumpwork. **Interfacing** is a fabric stiffener available in different thicknesses. We have used a firm, heavy-weight grade for raising flat surfaces. Interfacing can be coloured with fabric paints. **Felt** can also be used for padding. Layers can be built up to give a domed appearance to the shape, or by stuffing a single layer of felt with toy stuffing. Use a wool felt, as acrylic felt is too rigid for small pieces of stumpwork.

We have incorporated **fine copper wire** under the top stitching of some of the pieces of needlelace and around the freestanding embroidery to allow them to be bent into shape. **Paper-covered wire** wrapped with stranded cotton has been used to form flower stalks and birds' legs.

To introduce a different texture into the embroidery, we have used a very soft **gloving leather** for the heron's and wader's bodies. The log cabin and the fence have been made from cut and painted **balsa wood** and **lime wood**, and **cotton fibres** have been used for the snow.

Painting equipment

We have used **watersoluble crayons** to colour the background fabrics and the wood used for the log cabin and fence. The coloured background is then painted over with a **large paintbrush** dampened with clean water to blend the paint. **Fabric paints** have been used to paint the organza, noil and chiffon, and **acrylic paint** for the heron's markings. Both were applied using **small** and **medium-sized paintbrushes**. It is useful to have some **kitchen roll** to hand for mopping up spills and removing excess paint.

Other equipment

Pressed-paper egg boxes, when cut, shaped and painted, make realistic rocks, which surround the pond in the lower half of the picture. **PVA glue** is used to secure the threads when wrapping wire and to glue the balsa wood and lime wood together. We use **cocktail sticks** to push toy stuffing into a felt pad, and to manipulate very small elements. You need a **heavy-duty craft knife**, a **small craft knife** and a **cutting mat** for cutting the balsa wood and lime wood when making the log cabin and the fence; a **drawing pen**, **pencil** and **eraser** for sketching on to **paper** and for transferring the patterns and templates on to **tracing paper**; a **gold gel pen** for outlining the templates on the background fabric; **self-adhesive, transparent plastic** to form the protective layer on needlelace pads; and **surgical tape** to pad out the frog's thighs, under the needlelace.

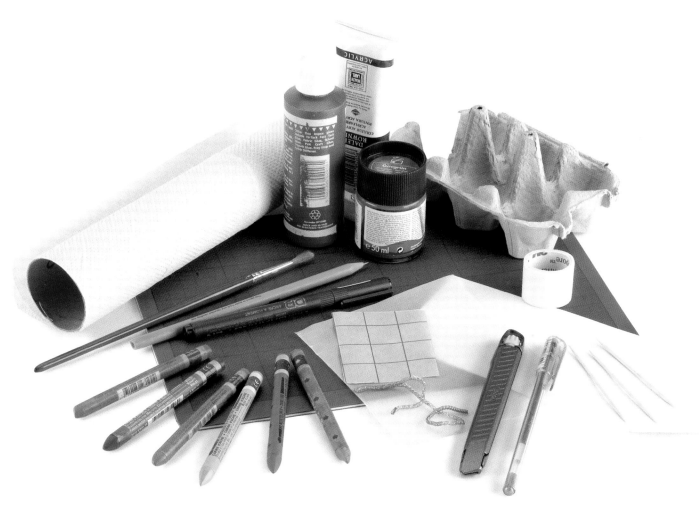

Embroidery stitches

This section provides demonstrations of the more complicated stitches used in the embroidery. Diagrams are provided at the back of the book on pages 78–79 for easy reference. Although all of the stitches shown in this book are technically correct, they have been adapted for use in stumpwork. For instance, before working long and short stitch, you should place an outline stitch around the shape first to give it a crisp edge. This outline stitch has been omitted from the deer, stag and squirrel to give them a furry appearance.

All the demonstrations on pages 14–21 are worked in stranded cotton, though on the embroidery we use silk thread as well.

Tip

Although we use fine silk for some of the stitches on the embroidery, all of them can be worked in six-stranded cotton if you prefer.

Back stitch

Used to outline the dragonfly's wings and the autumn tree. In both cases it is used to support the filling stitches (see pages 14 and 79).

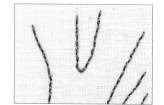
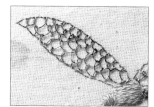

Up and down stitch

Used for the grass in the autumn scene (see pages 14 and 78).

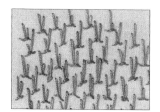
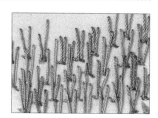

Long and short stitch

A traditional filling stitch, used to make the deer's, stag's and squirrel's fur (see pages 15 and 78).

Padded satin stitch

A raised filling stitch, used to make the snowdrop flowers and the dragonfly's body (see page 16).

Satin stitch

A filling stitch, used for the daffodil petals and the sheep's hooves. Follow the instructions for the top layer of padded satin stitch on page 16. (See also page 78).

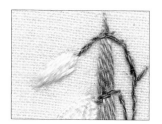

French knots

A versatile stitch, used to make the catkins, the sheep's fleeces, the spots on the frog's body, the weeds growing along the bottom of the wall, and the leaves on the autumn tree. Alter the size and texture of the stitch by varying the number of twists you make around the needle and the thickness of the thread (see pages 17 and 78).

Fly stitch

Used to make the sheep's mouths (see pages 17 and 79).

Needle-woven picot stitch

Used to make the freestanding daffodil petals and leaves, and the ferns (see pages 18 and 78).

Turkey knot stitch

A beautiful textured stitch, used to make the grassy bank, the centre of the lily flower and the squirrel's tail (see pages 19 and 79).

Padded raised chain band stitch

A textured filling stitch. It is usually worked in one direction, but here we have worked it in two directions to give more texture. Used to fill the trunk of the blossom tree (see pages 20 and 79).

Stem stitch

Used to make the daffodil and snowdrop stems, and the snowdrop leaves. Making three or four lines of stitches close together gives the leaves a slightly textured look (see page 79).

Stab stitch

Used to attach felt padding, slips and other elements to the embroidery (see page 78).

Back stitch

Back stitch has been used to outline the dragonfly's wings and the autumn tree on the background fabric. Use a No. 9 embroidery needle, and make small, evenly worked stitches. On the dragonfly's wings, use a single strand of metallic thread, and make the stitches large enough to work single Brussels stitch in to.

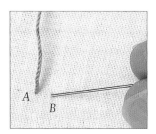

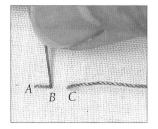

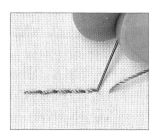

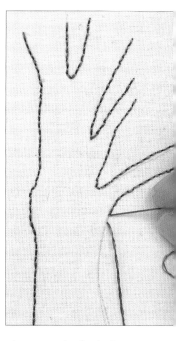

1. Bring the thread up through the fabric (A) and take it back down a short distance to the right (B).

2. Pull the thread through to form a short straight stitch. Work the next stitch in the opposite direction, bringing the thread up to the right of the first stitch (C), and taking it back down at B. Make sure this stitch is the same length as the first one.

3. Work subsequent stitches in the same way as the last, keeping the stitch length constant.

The tree on the finished embroidery was outlined in back stitch using two strands of six-stranded cotton.

Up and down stitch

This stitch has been used to make the grass in the autumn scene. We used two strands of six-stranded cotton in an embroidery needle, though in the demonstration below we have used only a single strand for clarity.

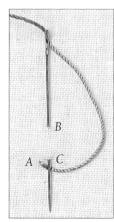

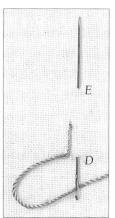

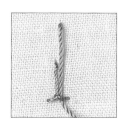

1. Begin by bringing the thread through to the front of the fabric at A. Take the thread down at B and back up just to the right of A at C, looping the thread under the needle.

2. Pull the thread through to form a stitch. Take the needle down just to the right at D, and bring it back up at E.

3. Pull the thread through and form a loop. Pass the needle through the loop.

4. Pull the thread through the loop and take the needle down just to the right of C to finish the stitch.

Long and short stitch

This is a useful filling stitch that can be adapted to any shape by varying the lengths and angles of the stitches. We used this stitch to make the deer's, the stag's and the squirrel's fur, using a No. 9 embroidery needle and one strand of six-stranded cotton (though two strands have been used in the demonstration below). To give the impression of fur, each stitch was passed through the middle of the stitch above, giving the surface of the embroidery a slightly irregular appearance.

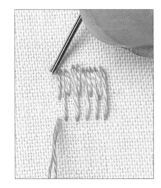

1. Make a single, long stitch and place a short stitch either side of it. Make sure the stitches are as close together as possible.

2. Work alternate long and short stitches outwards from the centre of your work.

The deer was worked using one strand each of light brown and cream six-stranded cotton.

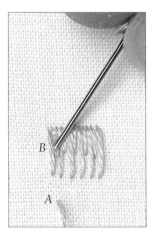

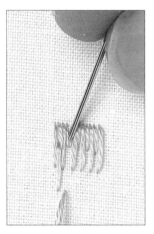

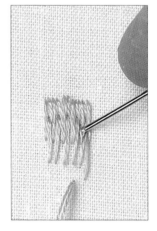

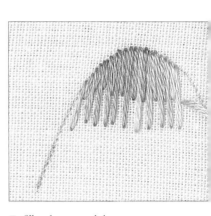

3. Start the next row below the first short stitch on the left, at A. Work a long stitch from A to B, taking the thread down a little way into the short stitch so that you split the thread.

4. Make another long stitch under the next short stitch along. Keep the lengths of the long stitches constant, unless you are filling an irregular shape.

5. Complete the second row. Begin the third row on the right, below the first long stitch in the first row. Work a long stitch as you did in step 3, and continue to the end of the row.

To fill a shape, work long stitches backwards and forwards across your work, varying the length, direction and colour as required.

Padded satin stitch

This is a traditional filling stitch, worked in layers to give a slightly raised appearance to your work. We used padded satin stitch to work the snowdrop flowers, using a single strand of 100/3 silk and a No. 9 embroidery needle. The stitch comprises three layers of satin stitch, each sewn in a different direction.

The snowdrop. Two needlelace petals have been attached to one of the flowers for a more realistic effect.

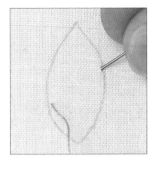

1. Work the first layer of stitches at a 45° angle across the shape, starting in the middle and working left to right. Position the needle just within the outline each time you take it through the fabric.

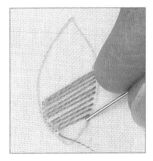

2. Lay each stitch as close as possible to the previous one, and parallel to it. Work down towards the base of the shape.

3. When you have filled the lower part of the shape, pass the thread through just above the first stitch you laid and begin to fill the top part.

4. Begin the second layer, placing the first stitch horizontally across the centre of the shape. Pass the needle through the outline this time, rather than just within it, and work from left to right as before.

5. Work one half of the shape first, then the other half.

The second layer of satin stitch.

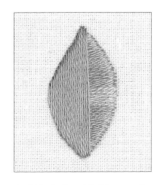

6. Work the third layer of padded satin stitch at right angles to the second, this time covering the outline by passing the needle through just outside it.

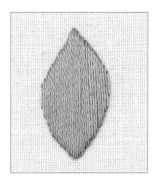

The third layer of satin stitch.

French knots

French knots have been used to make the catkins, the sheep's fleeces, the spots on the frog, the weeds growing along the base of the wall and the leaves on the autumn tree. You can vary the size and texture of the stitch by altering the thickness of the thread, the number of times you twist the thread around the needle, and how tightly you pull the thread to form the stitch. For example, the catkins were made using tight, neat stitches, and for the sheep's fleeces the stitches were made looser and less regular. We have used a No. 7 embroidery needle throughout.

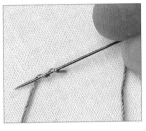

1. Bring the thread up through the fabric, hold it taut and wind the needle around the thread twice. For a smaller knot, wind the needle around the thread only once.

2. Keep the thread taut and pass the needle back through the fabric close to where it came up.

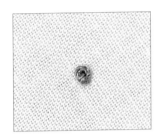

3. Release the thread when the needle has gone through the fabric and pull the knot tight.

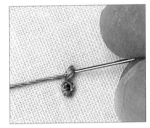

4. Make the next knot as close as possible to the first.

Fly stitch

This simple stitch was used to make the sheep's mouths. We have used a No. 9 embroidery needle and a single strand of six-stranded cotton.

The sheep's face. The mouth and eyes have been sewn on using a single strand of dark brown six-stranded cotton.

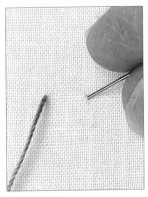

1. Bring the needle up through the fabric and take it back down to create the top of the 'V'.

2. Draw the thread into a loop and bring the needle back up inside the loop at the point of the 'V'.

3. Tighten the thread and take a small stitch over the point of the 'V' to secure it.

Needle-woven picot stitch

This stitch has been used to make the daffodil petals and leaves, and the ferns on the water's edge. Use a ballpoint needle to weave the thread through the three foundation stitches. The width of the top of the 'V' formed by the first three stitches, and the position of the pin, determine the width and length of the final shape.

The daffodil leaves were sewn straight on to the background fabric, whereas the ferns were sewn on to organza first, then cut out and attached to the background.

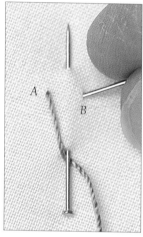

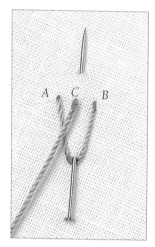

1. Insert a pin in the fabric as shown. Bring the needle up on one side of the pin (A) and take it back down on the other (B), looping the thread around the pin to form a 'V' shape.

2. Pull the thread through, and bring the needle back up halfway between the two points of the 'V' at C.

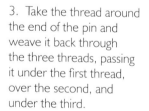

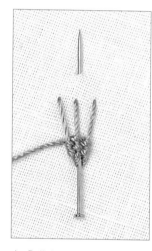

3. Take the thread around the end of the pin and weave it back through the three threads, passing it under the first thread, over the second, and under the third.

4. Pull the thread through and continue to weave backwards and forwards across the shape.

5. Weave to the end of the shape and take the thread through to the back of the fabric. Bring the needle up to start the next picot; otherwise secure the thread with two back stitches.

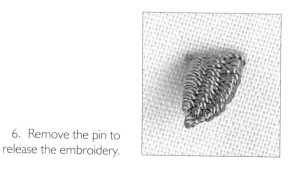

6. Remove the pin to release the embroidery.

Turkey knot stitch

We used turkey knot stitch, worked using three strands of six-stranded cotton and a No. 9 embroidery needle, to make the grassy bank, the centre of the lily flower and the squirrel's tail. This is a useful, decorative stitch that can be varied by altering the lengths of the loops – very small loops, when cut, will have a velvety texture, whereas long loops will have a more fluffy appearance.

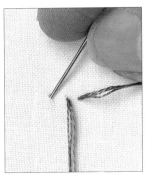

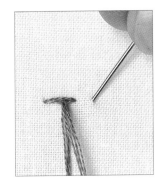

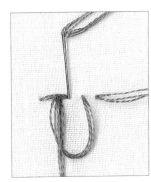

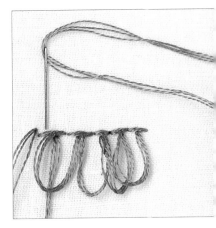

1. Take the thread through to the back of the fabric leaving a tail approximately 50mm (2in) long. Bring it back up a little way to the right, then pass the needle back down the same distance to the left.

2. Pull the thread through to form a stitch. Bring the needle up in the centre of the stitch, then take it back down a little way to the right.

3. Form a loop, then bring the needle up just to the right of the loop and back down at the right-hand edge of the first stitch.

4. Continue along for the required distance, then take the thread across the back of your work and start the next row of stitches just above the first.

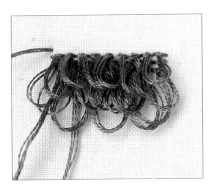

5. Work as many rows as required to achieve the right texture. Cut through the tops of the loops and tease the threads to create a fluffy appearance.

The grass on the finished embroidery was created by working twelve rows of turkey knot stitch using a variegated thread.

19

Padded raised chain band stitch

This is a lovely textured filling stitch which is usually worked in one direction but, for extra texture, can be worked up and down the bands. For the blossom tree, we have used a No. 9 embroidery needle and two strands of stranded silk, though in the demonstration below we have used only one strand of thread for clarity.

Begin by laying a base of chain stitch worked in rows, then lay bands across the shape and work a second layer over the top. This stitch can be made unpadded by omitting steps 1 to 4.

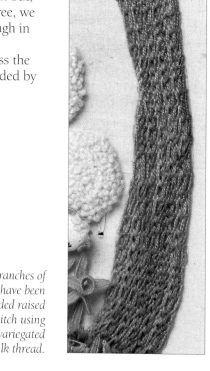

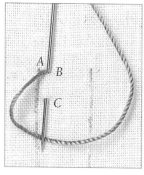

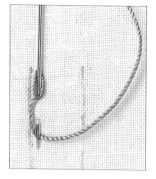

1. Bring the thread up through the fabric in the top left-hand corner of the shape (A). Take the needle back down just to the right (B), and up again a short distance below this (C), looping the thread under the needle as shown.

2. Pull the thread tight to form the stitch. Make the second stitch, taking the needle down inside the loop as close as possible to where it came up and looping the thread under the needle as before.

The trunk and branches of the blossom tree have been worked in padded raised chain band stitch using two strands of variegated silk thread.

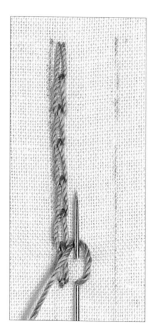

3. Continue working down the shape, turn, and work the next row of stitches from the bottom of the shape to the top.

4. Work rows of stitches up and down the shape until it is completely filled.

5. Rethread the needle and work couching stitches across the shape. Leave approximately 5mm (¼in) between stitches.

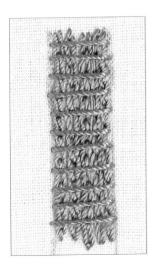

The completed couching stitches.

6. Change to a ballpoint needle and bring the thread up in the top left-hand corner of the shape, just above the first couching stitch. Loop the thread over and under the couching stitch, and tighten the thread.

7. Pass the needle under the same couching stitch, just to the right. Loop the thread under the needle and pull it taut to form a chain stitch.

8. Take the thread over and under the left-hand side of the second couching stitch, and form the next chain stitch in the same way as the first.

9. Continue working down the shape until you reach the last couching stitch. Pass the thread through to the back of the work. Bring the thread back up just to the right of the first row, and turn the embroidery round. Work back up to the top of the shape.

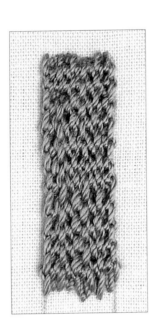

10. Work up and down the shape until you have completed the padded raised chain band stitch.

21

Needlelace techniques

Needlelace is a technique traditionally used in stumpwork to add texture and depth. The needlelace is worked on a separate pad over a cordonnet, which needs to be strong enough to support the filling stitches. A cordonnet consists of two strong threads, either a silk thread or fine crochet cotton, couched around the shape to be filled using a good quality pure cotton sewing thread. The cordonnet should have no joins, and more complex shapes require careful planning to avoid having to break and rejoin the thread, and to ensure that there are two threads on every part of the outline. The cordonnet can be stiffened by couching a length of fine wire in with the cordonnet threads. This allows the finished piece to be bent into freestanding shapes. By adding wire at this stage, rather than with the top stitching, the wire is hidden under the threads. The filling stitches are all versions of detached buttonhole stitch, and are conventionally worked in 100/3 silk thread or a single strand of six-stranded cotton.

When making a piece of needlelace to fit over a felt pad, it is imperative that you check the paper pattern first to make sure the finished embroidery will be the correct size; it is easier to adjust the pattern at this stage rather than to spend hours making a piece of needlelace that is too large or too small!

On the following pages we show you how to make a needlelace pad, plan the cordonnet for the small lily pad, and work a filling stitch. You will need a No. 9 sharps needle, a No. 9 ballpoint needle and one strand of variegated green six-stranded cotton.

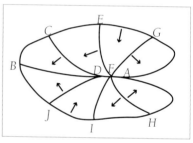

The template for the smallest of the three lily pads (actual size).

Needlelace pad

Make a sandwich starting with two or three layers of medium-weight calico, followed by the paper pattern, and finally a top protective layer of self-adhesive transparent plastic with the backing removed. Tack all the pieces together firmly. Make the pad large enough to accommodate either a single shape, or several smaller pieces. In the latter case, it is best to complete all the shapes on the pad before releasing any of them.

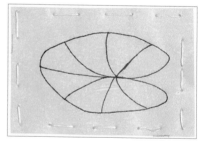

The needlelace pad for the lily pad.

The fish, the swan, the frog, the heron's wing and the lily have all been made using needlelace. Full instructions and patterns are provided later in the book.

Making the cordonnet

It is essential that the cordonnet stays intact when the needlelace is released from the backing fabrics. Take time to plan the layout properly so that you can build the cordonnet from a continuous length of thread. Use the full-size pattern to estimate the length of thread required – lay the thread along the lines on the diagram, double this length of thread and add a small extra allowance. For the small lily pad, you will need 830mm (33in) of thread.

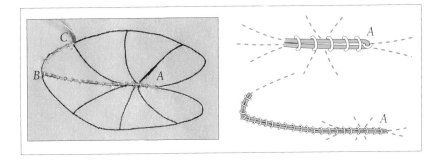

1. Fold the length of thread in half and lay the looped end over point A, at the end of the main vein. Using a No. 9 sharps needle with a single length of sewing thread, secure the loop with a single stitch worked from inside outwards. Bring the sewing thread back up on the design line, approximately 3mm (¹/₈in) from A, and make a stitch over the cordonnet threads. Continue couching around the outline until you reach the next leaf vein (point C).

Tip

A poor foundation will result in a disappointing piece of needlelace. Make the couching stitches small, firm and neat, and approximately 3mm (¹/₈in) apart. Put in an extra stitch on corners and sharp points; the more stitches you put in the less distortion you will get when making the filling stitches. If the couching thread runs out before you have finished the cordonnet, take the thread to the back of the needlelace pad and secure it with three or four stitches, then start a new length.

2. At C, separate the cordonnet threads and take one thread down the vein to D, catching it down in one or two places along the design line to hold it in position.

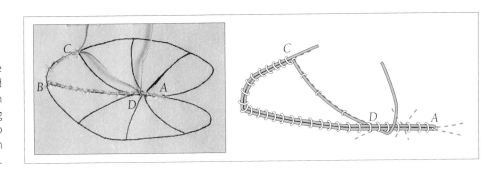

3. At point D, take the thread under and over the threads that are already couched down, lay it back down alongside the single thread, then couch down both threads to C.

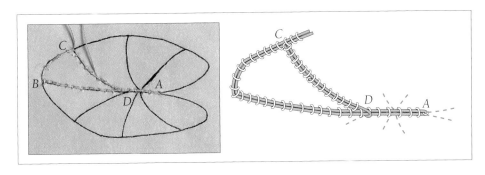

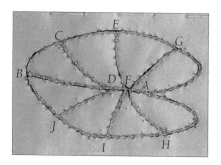

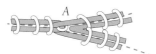

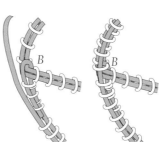

Passing the thread through the start loop, A.

4. Continue couching around the outer edge. Make branches at E–F and G–F. As you pass the start loop at A, take one of the threads through the loop, then continue round to H, making branches at H–F, I–F and J–D.

5. After completing the branch J–D, separate the threads and take one thread towards B (see far left diagram). Take it under and over the cordonnet at B and lay it back towards J, putting in two or three couching stitches to hold it on the design line. Couch down the other thread alongside the existing ones (as in the right-hand diagram on the left), taking it a short distance towards C. Fasten off the couching thread on the back of the pad, then trim away any excess cordonnet threads.

Filling stitches

Three filling stitches have been used in this book: single Brussels stitch, corded single Brussels stitch and up and down stitch. The filling stitches do not pass through the layers of the needlelace pad, but are worked over and supported on the cordonnet. Joins in the filling thread can only be made at the end of a row, so you must ensure that you have sufficient thread to work a full row of stitches. A good guide is always to have four times the length of the row you are working on. Use a No. 9 or 10 ballpoint needle, and either a 100/3 silk thread or one strand of six-stranded cotton. Always leave long tail threads when working the filling stitches – these can later be used to attach the needlelace to your embroidery.

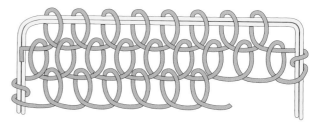

Single Brussels stitch

Start this stitch with a row of buttonhole stitches across the cordonnet. The spacing of this foundation row of stitches governs the texture of the finished piece: use loose stitches for an open texture; tight ones for a dense texture. Subsequent rows of stitches are looped into those above.

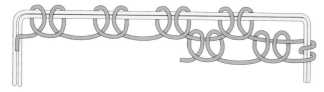

Up and down stitch

This stitch is made up of groups of two stitches. Begin by making a normal buttonhole stitch. Form the second stitch by taking the needle upwards under the cordonnet, pulling the thread through, then taking the needle downwards under the loop formed between the two stitches. Leave a space wide enough for two more stitches and continue along the row. For the second row, you can either lay a 'cord' across the space and repeat row 1, working the pairs of stitches into the loop and under the cord of the previous row, or work pairs of stitches into the loops left between those in the previous row.

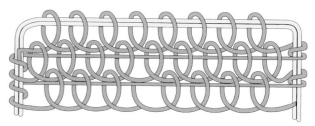

Corded single Brussels stitch

This stitch is worked in much the same way as single Brussels stitch except that, at the end of each row of buttonhole stitches, the thread is laid back across the work as a 'cord'. The next row of stitches is then worked round this cord and the loops in the previous row.

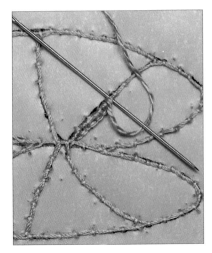

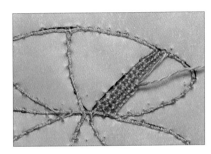

1. Begin to fill one segment of the lily pad with corded single Brussels stitch. Secure the end of the thread to the cordonnet by passing it under a few of the couching stitches, and work a row of evenly spaced buttonhole stitches across the vein. Do not pull the stitches too tight, as in the next row you must work through their loops.

2. When you reach the end of the row, take the needle and thread under then over the two cordonnet threads twice. Lay the thread back across the row as a cord and work back across the shape, working one buttonhole stitch round the cord and through each loop of the previous row. Whip the thread round the cordonnet again and work the next row. Continue working back and forth across the shape until the area is filled. Secure the last row of stitches by whipping each loop to the cordonnet, as shown in the diagram opposite.

3. Fill each segment of the lily pad. Use up and down stitch in two of the segments; up and down stitch is a more open, lacy stitch that breaks up the solidity of the corded single Brussels stitch.

Whipping a thread to the cordonnet.

Finishing

Needlelace is traditionally finished with a raised outer edge. This is achieved by top stitching. Only edges that are freestanding, such as the bottom edge of the swan's wing, require top stitching; other edges are stab stitched to the background fabric. Top stitching can also be used to highlight a surface detail, such as the veins on the lily pad. Once the top stitching is complete, remove the needlelace from the pad.

Tip

Fine wire can be added under the top stitching, allowing the edge to be sculpted.

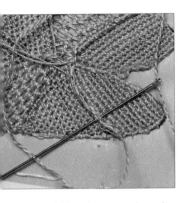

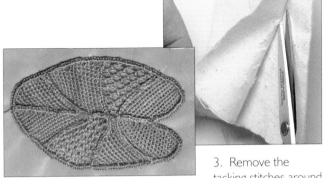

1. Using the same thread as the filling stitches, lay two threads along the veins of the lily pad, and attach them using closely worked buttonhole stitches.

2. Complete the top stitching along each of the veins, and around the outer edge of the lily pad.

3. Remove the tacking stitches around the outside of the pad, fold apart the last two layers of calico, then use fine-pointed scissors to snip through the stitches.

4. Remove the needlelace, and use tweezers to remove any remaining couching threads.

The embroidery

In common with traditional stumpwork, the embroidery is built up in layers, starting with the painted background and finishing with the attachment of raised elements, which are made on separate pieces of fabric, and needlelace.

We begin by showing you how to paint the background fabric, how to transfer the design to the fabric, and how to complete the background embroidery. The book is then divided into four sections – one for each season – which you can either work your way through from beginning to end, or dip into and select the elements you want to work on in whatever order you choose. (Remember, of course, that you need always to work from the back of the embroidery towards the front.) Alternatively, you may wish to adapt the design to produce four smaller, separate embroideries, one for each season.

The embroidery is worked on lightweight calico with a backing of medium-weight calico, secured in a 460mm (18in) embroidery hoop, sometimes known as a quilting hoop. All the stitching will pass through both layers of calico. You will also need a 150mm (6in) hoop, a 255mm (10in) hoop and a 305mm (12in) hoop to make some of the smaller, separate elements. All the materials and equipment you need are listed at the start of each section, and the templates, needlelace patterns and instructions for making the more complicated cordonnets are provided at the back of the book.

When you are working on your embroidery, make sure your hands are clean and do not put on too much hand cream as this can mark the fabric. Always cover the embroidery with a clean cloth when you are not stitching, and do not place drinks such as tea or coffee near the embroidery in case you accidentally spill them!

The main template

The purpose of the main template is to help you position the various elements on the embroidery. Only the basic outlines are included, as any detail would be covered by the stitching.

 You will need to begin by making a full-size copy of the template, shown below. If you have access to a computer scanner, scan in the drawing below and enlarge it two-and-a-half times. Print it out as 'tiles' on to A4 paper and join the pieces together with sticky tape. Alternatively, take it to your local print shop and have it printed on A2 paper, at two-and-a-half times the size shown below. The full-size circle should be 410mm (16¼in) in diameter.

Getting started

In this section we describe how to prepare the background for your embroidery, before adding the main elements. If you intend to produce a smaller embroidery, based on one of the four seasons, you will need to adapt the quantities and sizes of materials as appropriate.

You will need a large, flat surface to work on, in a well-lit area, and a comfortable chair. If you prefer to use a stand, you may need two to provide adequate support for the embroidery.

Painting the background

We used watersoluble crayons to colour the background fabric. Use horizontal strokes and the flat side of the 'point' of the crayon to lay the colour on to the calico. When using two or three colours, lay the colour in the spaces that are left rather than on top of previous colours, then mix them after all the colours are in place.

Materials

460mm (18in) embroidery hoop, with a bound inner ring
150mm (6in) embroidery hoop
Silk frame, 380mm (15in) square, and pins
Large pair of embroidery scissors
No. 9 embroidery needle, No. 9 sharps needle, No. 9 ballpoint needle and a darning needle
Lace pins and berry-head pins
Main template (full-size)
Full-size templates for the water and grass
Needlelace pad(s) for the freestanding snowdrop petals and dragonfly wings
Medium-weight calico, 610mm (24in) square
Lightweight calico, 610mm (24in) square
Silk organza, 410mm (16¼in) square
Silk chiffon, 410mm (16¼in) square
Silk noil, 410mm (16¼in) square
Heavy-weight interfacing, 355 x 130mm (14 x 5in)
Six-stranded cotton in yellow and various shades of green
Variegated six-stranded cotton in grey-blue and green
Variegated stranded silk in brown-green
100/3 fine silk thread in white
Variegated metallic thread
Bullion thread in silver-blue
Sewing cotton
Fine copper wire
Blue-coloured fine copper wire
Watersoluble crayons in mid-blue, grey, red, dark green and light green
Fabric paints in blue and light green
Three or four paintbrushes in a range of sizes
Absorbent paper
Gold gel pen
Lightbox (optional)
PVA glue

1. Lay the lightweight calico on a hard, flat surface. Start painting by lightly marking in the edge of the winter sky using a mid-blue watersoluble crayon. Place the frame over the fabric as a guide.

2. Remove the frame and colour in the sky using light, horizontal strokes. Leave two patches only lightly covered so they can be filled with a second colour.

3. Lightly fill one patch with grey and the other with red.

4. Secure the calico in the frame to raise it off the surface, and dampen the sky using clean water applied with a large paintbrush. Use just enough water to ensure the colours blend.

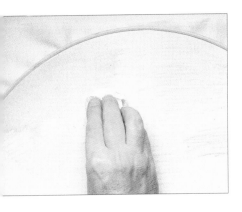

5. Dab out any excess colour (where it looks too dark) using a piece of absorbent paper.

6. Once the winter background has dried, remove the fabric from the frame and colour the other three seasons in the same way. Paint the backgrounds for autumn and spring using dark green and light green respectively, and paint the area in the centre of the fabric blue.

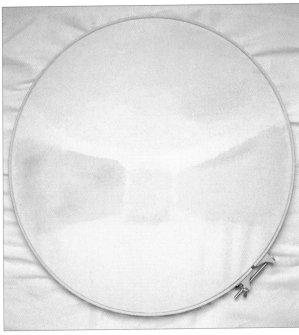

Tip

When painting the background, do not add water while the calico is resting on a hard surface, as the fabric will not dry and the paint will spread.

7. Adjust the colours by strengthening them where necessary using the watersoluble crayons, or softening them by dabbing with a paper towel. (This can be done while the calico is still in the frame.) Allow the paint to dry.

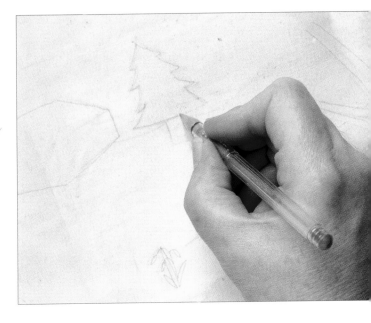

Transferring the design

Remove the calico from the hoop and centre it over the main template. You may wish to pin the two together to avoid the fabric slipping. Work either over a lightbox or by a sunny window so that the design shows clearly through the fabric. Using a gold gel pen, carefully trace over the outlines on the paper template.

Place the painted calico with the gold outlines on top of the piece of medium-weight calico, and mount the two layers of fabric in the hoop ready to begin the embroidery.

The background embroidery

Embroider the trunk of the blossom tree, the petals, stems and leaves of the daffodils on the right-hand side of the picture (the trumpets, and more freestanding daffodils, will be added later), the snowdrop and the dragonfly in the centre, and the grass on the left.

Daffodils

Begin by working the stems in stem stitch, following the lines transferred on to the background fabric. Use a No. 9 embroidery needle threaded with two strands of light green six-stranded cotton. Work the three petals of each flower that are drawn on to the background in satin stitch using one strand of yellow cotton. The other three petals are needle-woven picots, approximately 5mm (¼in) long, worked using a

ballpoint needle directly on to the background fabric, and placed between the existing petals. The leaves are also needle-woven picots, worked straight on to the background using a single strand of light green six-stranded cotton, and varying in length up to approximately 20mm (¾in).

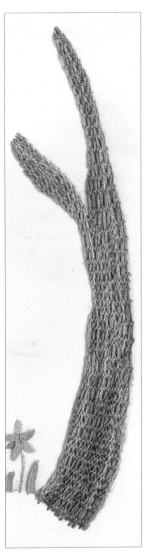

Grass

Randomly work three areas of grass (refer to the photograph on page 30). It does not matter if some grass is later covered by the deer, tree or rocks. Use up and down stitch, in various lengths, worked with two strands of variegated green six-stranded cotton and an embroidery needle.

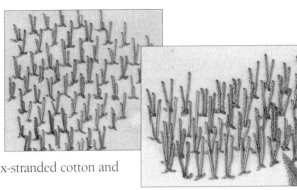

Snowdrop

Work the leaves as four rows of stem stitch, worked closely together, using an embroidery needle and one strand of mid-green six-stranded cotton. Next work the stems as a single row of stem stitch using a darker green thread. The petals are padded satin stitch worked with one strand of white 100/3 fine silk and and an embroidery needle.

Tree trunk

The trunk of the blossom tree is worked in padded raised chain band stitch. Work up and down the length of the tree for added texture, using two strands of variegated brown-green stranded silk and an embroidery needle.

Dragonfly

Use padded satin stitch for the body and head, worked with one strand of variegated grey-blue six-stranded cotton and an embroidery needle. Outline the two wings in back stitch using variegated metallic thread, and fill them with single Brussels stitch using the back stitch instead of a cordonnet for support. Cut a 30mm (1¼in) length of silver-blue bullion thread. Thread a ballpoint needle with one strand of variegated grey-blue six-stranded cotton, bring it through to the front of the fabric and pass it along the core of the bullion thread. Take it back through to the back of the fabric, then return it to the front of the work and secure the bullion thread with one or two couching stitches.

The water

For the water, use a piece of blue-painted organza overlaid with blue-painted chiffon.

  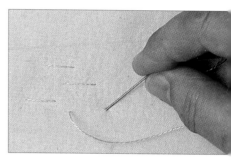

1. Attach the piece of silk organza to a 380 x 380mm (15 x 15in) silk frame. Using a large brush, wet the fabric first then apply a watery mix of blue fabric paint. Leave the paint to dry. Paint the silk chiffon in the same way.

2. Using the template on page 74, cut the shape of the water from each piece of silk. Position the organza on the background fabric at the bottom of the picture, overlay it with the chiffon and pin both pieces of fabric in place.

3. Stab stitch both layers to the background fabric, placing stitches only where they will eventually be covered by rocks or grass so they won't be visible on the finished embroidery. Create the ripples by placing single straight stitches randomly over the central part of the water. Use a single strand of grey-blue six-stranded cotton.

The grass

For the grass at the bottom of the embroidery, cut a piece of interfacing using the template supplied on page 74 and paint it with light green fabric paint. Paint an area of silk noil that is slightly larger than the template using the same colour. Allow both to dry.

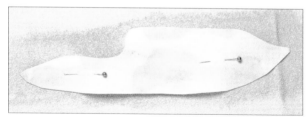

1. Pin the interfacing face down to the wrong side of the green-painted noil using berry-head pins.

2. Cut around the interfacing, leaving a 20mm (¾in) border.

3. Make snips in the border, cutting up to the edge of the interfacing, fold over the tabs and stick them down using PVA glue.

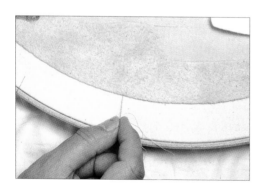

4. Attach the grass to the background fabric using stab stitches.

Completing the snowdrop and dragonfly

The snowdrop and dragonfly, which lie in the centre of the embroidery, can now be completed. Alternatively, you may prefer to do this later, incorporating them into one of the seasons, as both elements are made of needlelace and are very fragile; attach the dragonfly's wings as the last stage of summer, and the needlelace snowdrop petals at the end of spring. The patterns for these are provided on pages 70 and 71.

Snowdrop

The freestanding snowdrop petals are very delicate, and care must be taken when attaching them to the background fabric. They are made in needlelace, using one strand of 100/3 fine silk. Couch a fine wire around the outside with the cordonnet, and fill the shape using corded single Brussels stitch.

Attach the completed petals by making a small hole in the fabric at the top of the lower left-hand stem with a darning needle, and passing the wires through to the back of the work. Bend the wires so they lie along the back of the flower. Take the tail threads from the needlelace through to the back of the fabric and use them to overstitch the wires in place.

The completed freestanding petals.

Dragonfly

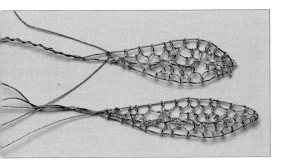

1. Begin by couching a thin, blue-coloured copper wire around the outside of each wing to stiffen it, working from the base of the wing, around the tip, and back to the base. Twist the two ends of the wire together. Using the variegated metallic thread, work buttonhole stitches around the inside of each wing, again starting at the base and working round the tip (see diagram below). Repeat once more, working the buttonhole stitches into the loops of the previous row. Work one more row from the base of the wing to the tip, then whip the thread through each buttonhole-stitch loop back to the base.

The filling stitches for the dragonfly's wings.

2. To attach the needlelace wings, make two adjacent holes in the embroidery, just below the existing wings, using a darning needle, and pass the wires and threads through to the back of the fabric. Use the threads to secure the wings by overstitching the wires in place. Lift and shape the wings so they stand proud of the background.

33

Some basic techniques

There are some techniques that you will use frequently. Mastering these will add to your confidence and greatly improve the quality of your finished embroidery.

Padding

Padding gives depth and texture to stumpwork, and there are various ways of achieving this. The padding used for the heron (see below), the swan and the wader consists of layered felt; the number of layers you use depends on the effect you wish to achieve. A single layer gives a slightly raised effect, whereas three layers give a domed appearance to the shape. Use a good-quality wool felt and sewing cotton, both in a similar colour to the element you are padding.

Position the first layer of felt over the roundest part of the shape you are padding, pin it in place, and secure it with neat, widely spaced stab stitches. The second layer is slightly larger than the first so that it fits neatly over the top. Use closer stitching to secure this layer. The third layer is a little larger again, and approximately 1mm (1/16in) smaller all round than the final shape. Attach it using neat, closely worked stab stitches.

Other types of padding used in stumpwork include interfacing, which gives a raised, hard surface (this has been used for the grass at the bottom of the embroidery), and toy stuffing, used to pad the sheep's heads. Other elements, such as the deer and the stag, are made on a separate piece of fabric, and the excess material is tucked underneath as they are attached to the background to create a padding.

Tip
When attaching a shape to a background using stab stitch, always bring the needle up at an angle from underneath the shape through to the top of the background fabric, and take it back down through the shape. This makes it easier to position the needle, and helps prevent damage to the edge of the shape, particularly when working with felt or leather.

1. Pin the first layer of padding to the lower part of the heron's body and then stab stitch it in place. It should lie approximately 5mm (1/4in) inside the gold outline.

2. Attach the second layer over the first in the same way, making sure it fits just within the gold outline. Secure it with six stab stitches spaced evenly around the shape, then fill in the gaps with more stitches.

3. Finally, secure the third and final layer of felt padding so that it sits just on the gold outline. As before, put in a few holding stitches first, then fill in the gaps.

Attaching slips

A slip is a small piece of embroidery that is made separately, and then attached to the main embroidery. The grassy bank, the sheep's bodies, the deer and the stag have all been made on fine calico, while the squirrel's tail has been first embroidered on to organza. Slips should be attached using the same thread with which you made them.

To give a slip a more rounded appearance, cut out the slip and gather the excess material underneath before attaching it to the background fabric, as shown below.

1. Secure the end of the thread, and place running stitches around the outside of the embroidery, approximately 5mm (¼in) from the edge. Leave a long tail thread. Do not secure the thread at this stage.

2. Cut out the slip, just outside the running stitches.

3. Holding the slip firmly, pull the tail thread to gather the fabric. The fabric is then hidden behind the slip. Secure the thread on the back of the fabric.

4. Position the slip on the main embroidery and hold it in position with pins.

5. Stab stitch the slip in place. Working around the edge of the fabric, put in a few securing stitches first, then fill in the gaps.

The second method of attaching slips is suitable for more intricate shapes, such as the deer, and involves simply tucking the excess fabric underneath the slip as you attach it to the background fabric.

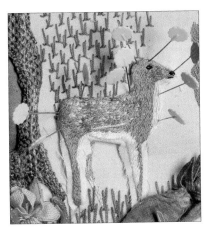

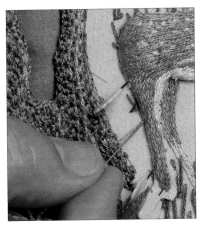

1. Cut out the slip, leaving a 10mm (½in) border around the outside. Snip into the border, cutting in as close as possible to the edge of the slip.

2. Pin the slip in place, tucking the excess fabric underneath. You may find it helpful to use a cocktail stick for this.

3. Stab stitch the slip on to the background, making sure the excess fabric remains neatly tucked underneath as you work.

Winter

Materials

Embroidery, general-purpose and large scissors
No. 9 embroidery needle, No. 9 sharps needle and No. 9 ballpoint needle
Lace pins
Full-size template for the padding for the large fir tree's trunk
Full-size template for the log cabin, copied on to A4 paper
Needlelace pad(s) for the two fir trees
Silk organza, 150mm (6in) square
Small piece of dark brown felt
2mm-thick lime wood planking, 5 x 915mm (¼ x 36in)
2mm-thick balsa wood, 75 x 305mm (3 x 12in)
Small quantity of toy stuffing
Cotton fibres
Six-stranded cotton in dark green, brown and white
100/3 fine silk thread in dark green and white
Silver metallic sewing thread
Sewing cotton
White bouclé wool
Watersoluble crayons in mid-brown, red and white
Small paintbrush
PVA glue
Cutting mat
Heavy-duty craft knife
Small craft knife
Nail file
Steel ruler
Cocktail stick
Tweezers
Damp sponge

The winter scene is possibly the easiest of the four seasons to make, and as it is at the top of the embroidery it seems logical to make it first.

We chose a snow scene, set against the painted winter sky, with a log cabin and two fir trees. The snow is carded cotton that has been teased out and held in place by stab stitches. The fir trees are made in needlelace. To represent snow resting on their boughs, the small tree is edged with top stitching using a white, fine silk thread, and the large tree is edged with white bouclé wool. Attach the smaller tree first, and then the snow. Next attach the larger tree, and finally add the log cabin, making sure the snow overlaps its base.

The needlelace patterns for the fir trees, and instructions for making the smaller tree's cordonnet, are provided on page 70. The template for the log cabin (given on page 77) includes cutting lines for the windows and door, and should be photocopied on to an A4 sheet of paper.

The fir trees and snow

Both the fir trees are made in needlelace using corded single Brussels stitch.

The small tree

The small tree is made in one piece, with the cordonnet running around the outside of each section of foliage (see page 70). It is made using a single strand of dark green six-stranded cotton, with white 100/3 silk used for the top stitching along the edges of the foliage. After releasing the needlelace from its pad, take all the loose threads through to the back of the work and use these to stab stitch the tree on to the background fabric.

The snow

Tease out a clump of cotton fibres, enough to lay all the snow in one go, and arrange it on the background. Make sure it covers the base of the small fir tree. Place stab stitches, worked with a single strand of white six-stranded cotton, randomly over the snow to hold it in place.

The large tree

The large tree is made in four separate parts, with a trunk that is applied over a layer of felt padding to give it a rounded appearance. Use the same dark green thread as you used for the small tree, and brown for the trunk.

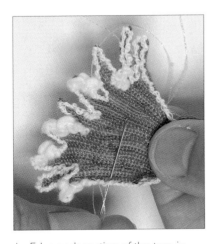

1. Edge each section of the tree in white bouclé wool to resemble snow, couched down using silver metallic sewing thread to give a hint of sparkle to the tree.

2. Cut out the felt padding for the trunk using the template on page 75 and stab stitch it in place. Pin then sew the trunk over the felt padding. Pin the lower section of the foliage in place and secure it with stab stitches along the two sides and the top edge. Use a silver metallic thread.

3. Attach the other three sections of the tree in the same way. At the top of the tree, take any tail threads through to the back of the fabric and secure them.

Log cabin

The logs for the cabin are made from lime wood, which is traditionally used for making model boats. All the logs are tapered to give a more realistic finish. You will construct the cabin on the template, placed on a cutting mat (don't worry if the paper sticks to the back of the cabin – it will help bind the model together). Keep a damp sponge to hand to remove any excess glue before it dries.

A simplified version can be made by replacing the sides of the cabin with balsa wood and painting in the details.

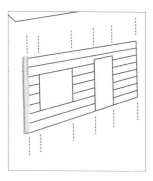  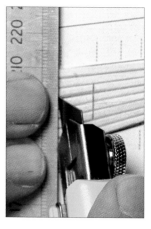

1. Starting with the front of the cabin, cut the left-hand corner piece from a strip of 2mm-thick lime wood. Round off the sides on one face using a nail file, cut it to the right length and place it on the template.

2. Cut eight 40mm (1½in) lengths of lime wood. Taper them using a nail file (or a small craft knife and steel ruler), and round off the corners on one face.

3. Dip the widest end of one of the logs in PVA glue, lie it along the top edge of the wall, and push it firmly against the corner piece to secure it. Apply glue to the rest of the logs and position them in the same way. Let the glue dry and trim them to the right length.

4. Aligning your ruler with the vertical guide lines, cut out the window and door with the heavy-duty craft knife.

   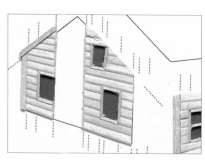

5. Cut the paper away from the window. To make the window frame, use thin strips of balsa wood (approximately 0.5mm thick and 1mm wide), apply PVA glue to them using a cocktail stick and manoeuvre them into position with tweezers.

6. For the door, cut approximately four strips of 1 x 1mm balsa wood, slightly longer than they need to be. Run glue down one side of each strip and slot them in place one at a time.

7. Trim off the excess wood at the bottom of the door with a craft knife.

8. For the side of the cabin you will need 16 tapered strips of lime wood, each 50mm (2in) long. Make it in one piece, attaching the logs following the same method you used for the front of the cabin. Cut out the windows and chimney following the guide lines. Attach the left corner post and, using a strip of balsa wood, the eave behind the chimney. Cut the paper away from the windows and fit the frames.

9. For the chimney, cut a 45 x 10mm (1¾ x ½in) piece of balsa wood, which is a little longer than it needs to be, and attach a narrow (2 x 2mm) strip to each side.

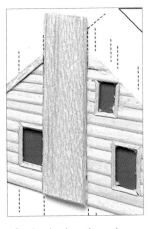

10. Apply glue along the two thin strips and secure the chimney in position.

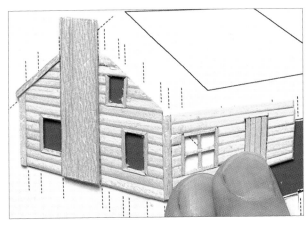

11. Cut out the front of the cabin using a small craft knife and glue it to the side.

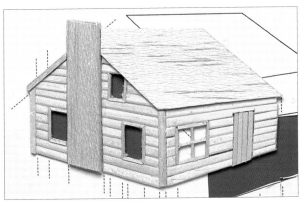

12. Cut out the first layer of the roof from 2mm-thick balsa wood using the template. Cut the second layer so that it is 2mm deeper and wider, and glue it on top of the first. Cut off the top left-hand corner to fit round the chimney. Make sure the roof fits neatly and cut away any excess wood with the large craft knife. Glue it in place using PVA glue.

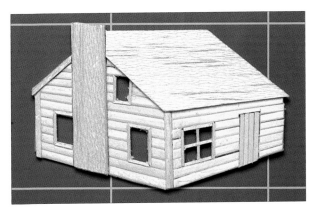

13. Cut the completed cabin away from the paper.

14. To complete the cabin, use watersoluble crayons to paint the logs brown and the chimney red, adding white lines to the chimney when the paint is dry to suggest brickwork. Glue a layer of organza behind the windows, and attach the cabin to the background using PVA glue. Make sure the snow overlaps the base of the cabin. Place a thin layer of cotton fibres on the roof, not forgetting the eave behind the chimney, stick it down with PVA glue, and push a small amount of toy stuffing into the chimney for smoke.

Spring

For this part of the embroidery, we have chosen elements traditionally associated with spring; grazing sheep and lambs, framed by golden daffodils, catkins and blossom. Here we introduce slips in the form of the sheep and lambs and the clumps of grass. We have used gloving leather for the sheep's faces and French knots for their fleece; the grass consists of turkey knot stitch. The catkin boughs and the blossom boughs (we have made two of each) are constructed separately before being attached to the background, the rocks are made from pressed-paper egg boxes, and the fence from balsa wood. Additional freestanding daffodils are added to the scene, and trumpets added to those already embroidered on to the background. All these elements together add texture and depth, which are enhanced by the use of variegated threads to make the tree trunk, the grass and the ferns.

Grassy bank

Many of the elements in this section have been made as slips before being attached to the background fabric. We have begun with the grass itself, which we have worked as four, progressively smaller, slips. Begin by securing a piece of lightweight calico in a small embroidery hoop, then work all four slips together before cutting them out and attaching them to the background fabric. The templates for the clumps of grass are provided on page 76.

Grass

1. Create the largest of the four clumps of grass by working twelve rows of turkey knot stitch using three strands of variegated green six-stranded cotton and a No. 9 embroidery needle. For the remaining three slips, work successively fewer rows.

2. Cut out the slips and gather the excess fabric underneath (see page 35). Cut through the ends of the loops of the turkey knot stitches using a pair of sharp scissors.

A completed clump of grass.

3. Pin the largest clump of grass to the background, at the base of the tree, and stab stitch it in place.

4. Attach the second clump alongside, to the left, followed by the remaining two, ending with the smallest clump.

41

Ferns

These are made separately on a piece of silk organza secured in a 150mm (6in) embroidery hoop. This fabric works well as a base for slips, as it is fine, easy to cut out, and virtually invisible when attached to the background fabric. Each fern is made up of four to six fronds, each approximately 16–18mm (¾in) long, worked in a tight circle, with the bases of the fronds overlapping.

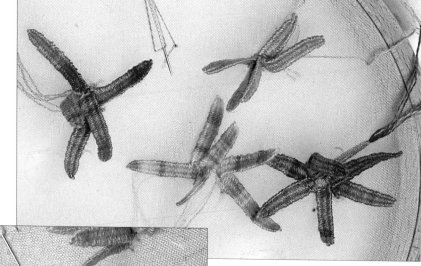

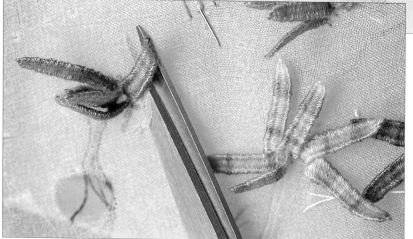

1. Sew seven ferns (or as many as you like) on to the organza using needle-woven picot stitch (see page 18). Use one strand of variegated six-stranded cotton in various shades of yellow, green, brown and red. Leave long tail threads with which to attach each fern to your embroidery.

2. Carefully cut out each fern, leaving a circle of organza around the base.

Tip

You may wish to make extra ferns and rocks (page 44) to use in the summer scene (see page 59).

3. Position each of the ferns on your embroidery, take the tail threads through to the back of the fabric and secure them.

Daffodils

You will need to make three or four freestanding daffodils, and enough trumpets for all of the flowers, including those embroidered on to the background (see page 30). The freestanding daffodil petals are made with 100/3 fine silk on a small piece of watersoluble fabric secured in a small embroidery hoop. Each flowerhead consists of five needle-woven picots, each approximately 5mm (¼in) long, worked in a tight circle.

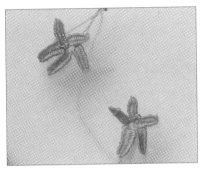

1. Make three or four groups of daffodil petals using needle-woven picot stitch. Use a single strand of 100/3 fine silk, in the same shade of yellow as the background daffodils.

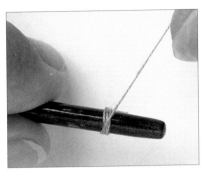

2. For the trumpets, begin by threading a needle with a single strand of yellow six-stranded cotton, and wind it three times around the end of a paintbrush.

3. Work one row of buttonhole stitch around the circle of threads.

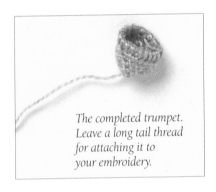

4. Work a further five rows of buttonhole stitch. Weave the thread through the last row of stitches, slip the stitching off the end of the paintbrush, and pull the thread tight to form a cup shape.

The completed trumpet. Leave a long tail thread for attaching it to your embroidery.

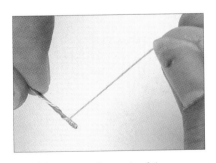

5. Make a stem for each of the freestanding daffodils. Take an 80mm (3¼in) length of paper-covered wire, dip the end in PVA glue and closely wrap a single strand of green six-stranded cotton around the first 5mm (¼in).

6. Cut out a ring of petals and dampen the watersoluble fabric to dissolve it away. Push the tip of a stem up through the centre of the flower. Make sure the green thread remains at the back so that you can use it to wrap round the rest of the stem.

7. Slip the trumpet over the tip of the wire and pass the thread through to the back of the flower. Continue wrapping the green thread around the wire and all the loose threads to form the stem. It should be approximately 20mm (¾in) long. Secure the green thread at the end with either a knot or a dab of PVA glue, leaving a long tail.

A completed daffodil.

8. Attach the freestanding daffodils to the background by slipping the ends of the stems behind the grass and oversewing them in place using the green thread. Attach the trumpets to the background flowers by passing the threads through to the back of the fabric and securing them.

Rocks

1. Cut out the shapes for the rocks from pressed-paper egg boxes.

2. Colour each rock using green and brown watersoluble crayons.

3. Apply water with a damp paintbrush to blend the colours.

4. Attach the rocks to the background by pushing them up underneath the grass a little way and stab stitching them in place.

5. To finish, push a clump of ferns (see page 42) into one of the crevices between the rocks, pass the thread through, pull it taut and secure it at the back of your work.

Fence

The fence is made of balsa wood, which is a soft wood that is easy to cut using a good, strong craft knife with a sharp blade. You will need a copy of the template on A4 paper, covered with transparent sticky tape. This will prevent the balsa wood from sticking to the paper when you glue the parts together. Work on a cutting mat, and use a damp sponge to wipe away any excess glue before it dries.

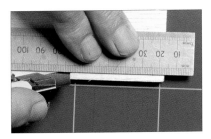

1. Begin by cutting a 4mm (¼in) wide strip from the balsa wood using a heavy-duty craft knife and a metal ruler.

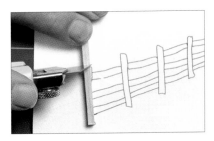

2. Lay it over the first fence post on the template and trim it to the correct length.

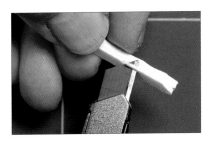

3. Give the wood a distressed look by randomly trimming thin slivers from the corners using a small craft knife. Always cut away from you.

4. Place the fence post on the template and cut three 2mm (⅛in) wide pieces of wood for the first three rails, making them slightly longer than required Give each of them a distressed finish, and trim the left-hand end off at a slight angle.

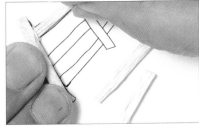

5. Dip the left-hand end of each rail in PVA glue and position the rails on the template, pushing them firmly against the first post.

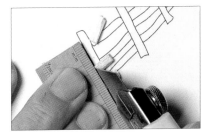

6. Trim the rails to the correct length by laying a ruler across them and cutting with the heavy-duty craft knife.

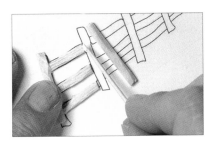

7. Make the next fence post, and apply glue to the right-hand ends of the rails using a cocktail stick to secure it.

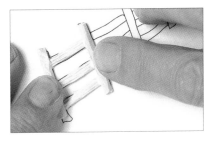

8. Fix the second post in place.

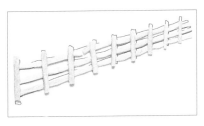

9. Complete the remainder of the fence in the same way. When all the glue has dried, scrape off the excess with the small craft knife.

10. Paint the fence using brown watersoluble crayon, allow it to dry and position it on your embroidery so that the lower edge of the bottom rails aligns with the gold line drawn on the background fabric, and the left-hand end is just to the right of the snowdrop. If necessary, trim the right-hand end of the fence so that it sits neatly against the tree trunk. Sew the fence in place by taking a stitch over each of the bottom rails, next to the fence posts.

Blossom

Each leaf and petal of the blossom bough is made individually in needlelace, the patterns for which are provided on page 71. You can make as many flowers and leaves as you like – we have made four large flowers, each with five petals; five medium-sized flowers with four petals each; four small flowers, also with four petals; twelve small leaves; and five large leaves. In addition, you will need three large leaves to hide the points at which you attach the boughs to the embroidery.

The instructions below are for a single blossom bough; you will need to make two altogether.

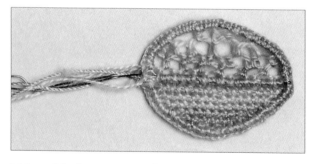

Make each leaf using variegated green six-stranded cotton. Couch a thin copper wire around the outside with the cordonnet, and along the central vein (see page 71). Fill one half of the shape using corded single Brussels stitch, and the other half using up and down stitch (see page 24). Leave tail threads of approximately 50mm (2in), and apply top stitching around the outside.

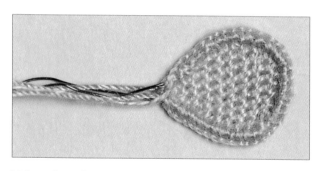

Make each petal using variegated pink six-stranded cotton. Couch a thin copper wire around the outside with the cordonnet, and fill the shape using corded single Brussels stitch. Leave tail threads of approximately 50mm (2in), and apply top stitching to the outside.

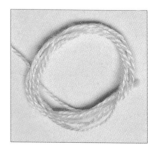

1. Make the stamens in the centre of each flower by first wrapping a 250mm (10in) length of cream six-stranded cotton around your forefinger to create several loops.

2. For the large flowers, group three petals together, right-side up, as shown in the photograph, and place the looped yellow thread on top of them. For the smaller flowers, use only two petals.

3. Lay two more petals on top, face down, and bind all the tail threads and wires together by wrapping a single green cotton thread around them to form the stems. Wind the thread down for approximately 10mm (½in), leaving the rest of the stem bare.

4. Arrange the petals to form the shape of the flower, and snip through the ends of the loops to make the stamens.

5. To form the blossom bough, work from the top of the bough downwards. Bind the top two flowers together first, then gradually bind in the other elements. Use the tail threads for binding, knotting them at the end to secure them. It does not matter in what order you combine the elements.

The complete blossom bough.

Catkins

The two catkin boughs are made in a similar way to the blossom boughs. We have made five catkins and five leaves for each one, though again you can make as many elements as you wish.

The catkins are made as freestanding elements, for which you will need two layers of lightweight calico supported in a small embroidery hoop. The leaves are needlelace, made in the same way as the blossom leaves, using the pattern for the small leaves on page 71.

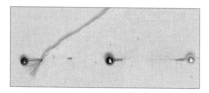

1. To make the catkins, insert three berry-head pins into the calico, 25mm (1in) apart, as shown above. Tie a 305mm (12in) length of cream six-stranded cotton around the left-hand pin.

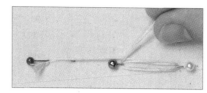

2. Take the cotton around the right-hand pin and wind it around this and the middle pin three times.

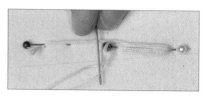

3. Separate off one strand of thread using the eye end of a No. 7 embroidery needle.

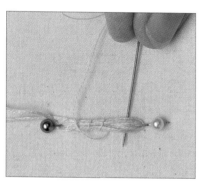

4. Thread the single strand through the needle and use it to bind together the wound threads.

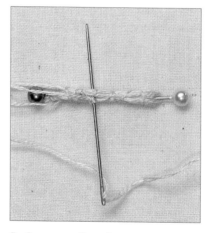

5. Separate off another two strands, thread them through the needle and work French knots over the surface of the bound threads.

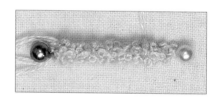

A completed catkin.

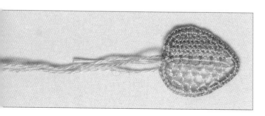

Make each leaf using a variegated green thread following the same method used for the small leaves on the blossom boughs (see page 46).

6. Begin to make the bough by dipping the end of a 100mm (4in) length of paper-covered wire in PVA glue. Wrap the first 10mm (½in) in green silk noil, then bind in the first catkin.

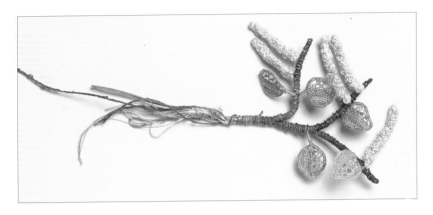

7. Continue down the branch for approximately 30mm (1 ¼in), binding in another catkin and a leaf. Work two other branches in the same way, one with two catkins and two leaves and the other with one catkin and one leaf. Bind in these other two branches, following the picture opposite, together with another single leaf, to create the bough.

Attaching the blossom and catkins

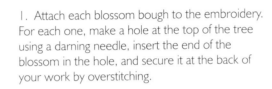

1. Attach each blossom bough to the embroidery. For each one, make a hole at the top of the tree using a darning needle, insert the end of the blossom in the hole, and secure it at the back of your work by overstitching.

2. Attach the catkin boughs, just below the blossom boughs, using the same method. Attach three large leaves to cover the places where the boughs pass through the embroidery. Attach the leaves by passing the stems through to the back and securing them with overstitching.

Sheep

The sheep's heads are made out of soft gloving leather, and the bodies are made using French knots. We worked the sheep's fleece in tapestry wool for a soft, woolly appearance; for the lambs' fleece we used two strands of six-stranded cotton. Make the bodies as separate slips on a piece of lightweight calico mounted in a small embroidery hoop. All the sheep's bodies can be made at the same time, on the same piece of calico. Similarly, all the heads can be made together, on another piece of fine calico.

When working with leather, always use a new, fine sharps needle, and avoid making unnecessary holes in the material.

Tip
If the sheep is looking down, use 'V'-shapes for the eyes; to make them look straight forward, turn the Vs on their sides, as shown opposite.

1. Cut out all the head shapes using the templates provided on page 77 and stab stitch them to the calico using a strand of six-stranded cotton. Sew from the chin up to one ear, then from the chin to the other ear. Place a single stitch just above each ear and leave the top of the head open. Do not stitch the ears down.

2. Stuff the head using toy stuffing. Push it in using the end of a cocktail stick.

3. Sew up the head and embroider the eyes and mouth using a single strand of dark brown six-stranded cotton. Use two straight stitches for each eye and a fly stitch for the mouth.

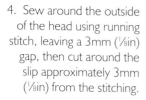 

4. Sew around the outside of the head using running stitch, leaving a 3mm (⅛in) gap, then cut around the slip approximately 3mm (⅛in) from the stitching.

5. Pull the running stitch tight so that the surplus calico goes up behind the head.

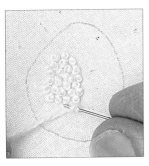

6. For the sheep's bodies, draw the outlines on to calico with a gold gel pen using the templates provided, and fill them with closely worked French knots. Use a No. 7 embroidery needle and two strands of cream six-stranded cotton for the lambs' fleece and one strand of tapestry wool, as shown above, for the adults.

7. Make the slips for the sheep's bodies in the same way as the heads (see steps 4 and 5).

A completed lamb's body.

8. Make each of the ram's horns by dipping the end of a 30mm (1¼in) length of paper-covered wire in PVA glue and wrapping it tightly with light brown six-stranded cotton.

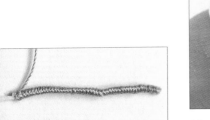

9. Bind approximately 20mm (¾in) of the wire, leaving 10mm (½in) bare. Knot the end of the thread, leaving a long tail with which to attach the horn to the ram's head.

10. Sew some French knots on top of the ram's head using the tapestry wool. Make a small hole just behind the ear. Bend the wire into a coil, dip the bare end in PVA glue and insert it into the hole. Attach the second horn in the same way.

11. Position the sheep's bodies on the background fabric and stab stitch them in place. Attach the sheep's heads, making sure they sit on top of the bodies and are not separate from them.

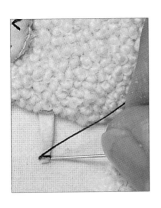

12. Cut out the sheep's legs from a piece of leather using the templates provided on page 77. Tuck them under the body and secure them with two small holding stitches. Sew on the hooves using satin stitch worked in a single strand of dark brown six-stranded cotton.

The completed sheep. Add some long stitches and French knots, using a single strand of green six-stranded cotton, to resemble grass.

Autumn

The predominant feature of the autumn scene is the magnificent tree on the left, made as a separate slip and embroidered using needlelace up and down stitch for the trunk and hundreds of French knots for the foliage. Rather than using a conventional needlelace pad, we have worked the trunk on calico with a back stitch outline to support the filling stitches. The wall is built from bricks made individually from calico-covered card, and the squirrel, deer and stag are made as slips, with long and short stitch for the fur.

Materials

255mm (10in) embroidery hoop
150mm (6in) embroidery hoop
Embroidery, general-purpose and large scissors
Nos. 7 and 9 embroidery needles, No. 9 sharps needle, No. 9 ballpoint needle and darning needle
Flower-head and berry-head pins
Full-size templates for the stones, wall, autumn tree, squirrel, deer and stag
Needlelace pad for the antlers
Three pieces of lightweight calico: 305mm (12in) square, 205mm (8in) square and 205 x 75mm (8 x 3in)
Silk organza, 205mm (8in) square
Small piece of light brown gloving leather

Six-stranded cotton in various shades of brown, pale cream and black
Variegated six-stranded cotton in brown-green, green and brown
Sewing cotton
Paper-covered wire
Watersoluble crayons in grey, green and brown
Medium-sized paintbrush
Gold gel pen
PVA glue
Black petite bead
Cocktail stick
Tweezers
Thin card
Black card

Wall

The first step is to paint a piece of lightweight calico measuring 205 x 75mm (8 x 3in), using watersoluble crayons in brown, green and grey, applied randomly for a mottled effect. Apply the colours first, then blend them using a damp paintbrush and allow the fabric to dry. Templates for the stones can be found on page 77; alternatively, simply cut them out by eye in a variety of shapes and sizes. You will need fifty to sixty rocks altogether.

1. Cut each rock shape from thin card, then place it on the back of the painted calico and cut around it leaving a 2mm (⅛in) border.

2. Snip in to the calico, up to the edge of the card.

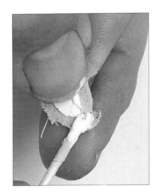

3. Apply PVA glue to the fabric using a cocktail stick and fold in the flaps.

4. When you have made enough rocks, cut out the background for the wall from black card using the template provided on page 77 and glue them on. Lay the rocks as close together as possible, as if you were building a real wall. Start on the right with the larger rocks and gradually incorporate more smaller rocks as you work towards the left. Alternatively, follow the pattern for the assembled wall provided on page 77.

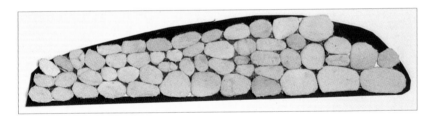

The finished wall.

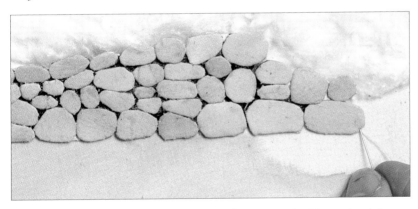

5. Trim off the excess card and attach the wall to your embroidery using stab stitching. Place the wall over the snow, not behind it.

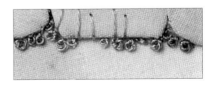

6. Sew French knots and long stitches along the base of the wall to represent weeds. Use variegated brown-green cotton thread.

Tree

Make the tree on a separate piece of lightweight calico, measuring 305mm (12in) square. Using a brown watersoluble crayon, paint an area approximately 225 x 125mm (9 x 5in). When the paint is dry, transfer the outline for the tree using the template on page 75. Place the calico in a 255mm (10in) embroidery hoop.

1. Back stitch around the outline of the tree trunk and branches using two strands of brown six-stranded cotton and a No. 9 embroidery needle. Fill the trunk and branches using needlelace up and down stitch (see page 24) worked using two strands of variegated brown six-stranded cotton and a ballpoint needle. Start at the base of the trunk, and work up and down the tree in rows. Fill the leafy part of the tree with French knots (see page 17). Work some using two strands of brown six-stranded cotton and some with two strands of variegated brown-green cotton, using a No. 7 embroidery needle.

2. Cut out the slip for the tree leaving a 10mm (½in) margin and attach it to your embroidery using stab stitch. Place only a few securing stitches at the top of the tree so that it lies gently over the snow, and attach the trunk firmly using closely worked stitches.

3. Working by eye, outline the tree roots using back stitch. Fill them using up and down stitch, as you did for the trunk. Add some more grass if necessary to blend the roots in with the background (see page 31).

Squirrel

The squirrel is made as two separate slips – one for the tail and one for the body. Templates for each are provided on page 77. Make the squirrel's body on a piece of lightweight calico and the tail on silk organza. The organza is finer than calico and lies more easily under the turkey knot stitching.

Tip

Make the squirrel, deer and stag from the same piece of 205mm (8in) square lightweight calico mounted in a 150mm (6in) embroidery hoop.

1. Embroider the top part of the body using a single strand of brown six-stranded cotton and a No. 9 embroidery needle. Change to a lighter brown for the middle part of the body and the front leg, and pale cream for the squirrel's chin and chest. Work in long and short stitch, starting at the nose and working backwards, following the curve of the body. To emphasise the back leg, change the direction of the stitches, working them up and down instead of across the shape. Sew on a black petite bead for the eye.

2. The tail is made using turkey knot stitch (see page 19). Work the loops in dense rows to make it soft and bushy.

3. Attach the squirrel's body close to the side of the tree using stab stitch, making sure that the surplus calico is tucked carefully underneath the body. Sew on the tail in the same way. For the ear, make a single chain stitch (consisting of a loop secured at the end with a small stitch) using two strands of cotton.

Deer

The deer is made on the same piece of lightweight calico as the squirrel and stag. The template is provided on page 75. We have used long and short stitch to fill the body, worked using a single strand of six-stranded cotton and a No. 9 embroidery needle. To give the impression of fur, pass each stitch through the middle of the stitch above for a slightly irregular finish.

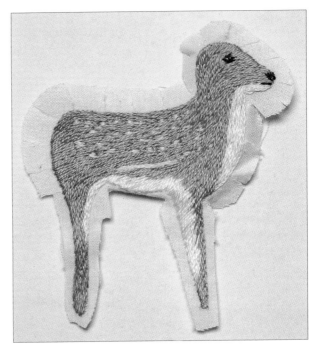

1. Begin by embroidering the cream-coloured markings on the deer's body. Use satin stitch for the spots and stem stitch for the line. Starting at the nose, work the head, neck, body and legs in long and short stitch, following the contours of the body. Use light brown thread for the main parts of the deer, and pale cream for the underside and inner parts of the legs. Finish by sewing on the eye, nose and mouth using satin stitch worked with a single thread of black six-stranded cotton.

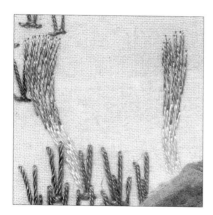

2. Embroider the legs on the background fabric using long and short stitch, first checking that they align correctly with the completed slip. Work the tops of the legs in light brown and the lower parts in pale cream. Add more grass to help them blend with the background.

3. Attach the deer to the background following the method described on page 35. Cut two ears from a piece of light brown gloving leather using the template provided and glue them in place using PVA glue. Use tweezers to help position them.

Stag

Make the stag in the same way as the deer, on the same piece of calico. Start by embroidering the spots and line along the side of the body using a single strand of pale cream six-stranded cotton and a No. 9 embroidery needle. Work the spots in satin stitch and the line in stem stitch. Return to the nose, and fill the head with long and short stitch worked from the nose outwards using a light brown thread. For the body and legs, work right to left, following the body's contours, using light brown for the main parts, and cream for the deer's chest, belly and the lower parts of its front leg. Finally, use satin stitch worked in a single black thread for the eyes and nose, and stem stitch for the shading under the head and the tail.

After completing the stag, cut it out from the calico and make sure it fits over the two legs outlined on the background. Embroider these two legs using long and short stitch. Attach the stag to the background fabric, turning the surplus material underneath as you work (see page 35).

Antlers

Though not worked in needlelace, we found the easiest way to make the antlers was on a needlelace pad. The templates are provided on page 75.

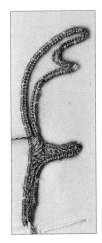

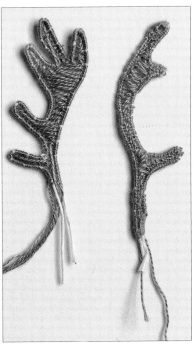

1. Couch a length of paper-covered wire over the design using white sewing cotton. Leave a tail of at least 25mm (1in).

2. Work buttonhole stitches over the wire, with the loops on the inside of the shape. Use a single strand of dark brown cotton and a ballpoint needle.

3. Make satin stitches across the shape, passing the thread through the buttonhole stitches on either side. Leave long tail threads.

The completed antler.

4. Complete both antlers and remove them from the needlelace pad.

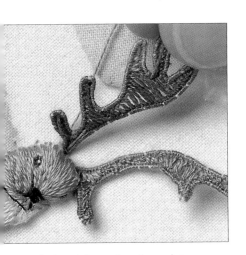

5. Insert the antlers through two holes made in the fabric using a darning needle. Pass the tail threads and wires through to the back of the work and use the threads to oversew the antlers in place.

6. Complete the stag by adding two ears, cut from light brown gloving leather using the templates on page 75.

Summer

This delightful scene covers the lower part of the embroidery, and includes a number of elements worked in needlelace, a traditional technique that has been used in stumpwork for hundreds of years. The swan, fish and frog are made entirely of needlelace, and the heron and wader are made of gloving leather, with needlelace wings. The picture is framed by the yellow needlelace irises on the left and the pink lily on the right. We have used machine stitching on the iris leaves, but the same finish can be achieved by handstitching if you do not have access to a sewing machine. Rocks and ferns border the pond, and mark the transition from spring to summer, and from summer to autumn.

The irises are composed of three different types of petal, and involve some new techniques that have not been used elsewhere: we show you how to change to a different colour thread; how to work with two needles; and how to create ring picots.

150mm (6in) embroidery
hoop and 255mm (10in)
embroidery hoop
Silk frame, 255mm (10in)
square, and pins
Embroidery, general-
purpose and large scissors
Nos. 7 and 9 embroidery
needle, No. 9 sharps
needle, two No. 9
ballpoint needles and a
darning needle
Berry-head and lace pins
Full-size templates for the
wader, fish, heron, swan,
frog and iris leaves
Needlelace pads for the
iris petals, wader's wing,
swan, swan's wing, fish,
frog, lily and heron's wing
Two pieces of silk organza,
610 x 305mm (24 x 12in)
and 205mm (8in) square
White felt, 305mm
(12in) square
White gloving leather,
130 x 75mm (5 x 3in)

Six-stranded cotton in
black, pink, pale green,
orange, white, yellow and
dark brown
Variegated six-stranded
cotton in light blue,
greens, browns and reds
100/3 fine silk thread in
yellow, white, orange,
black, grey, light blue and
mid-brown
Sewing cotton
Fine copper wire
Paper-covered wire
Black acrylic paint
Green fabric paint
Watersoluble crayons in
green and brown
Three paintbrushes (fine,
medium and large)
Gold gel pen
PVA glue
Two black and one silver
petite beads
Black seed bead
Pressed-paper egg boxes
Tweezers
Surgical tape

Rocks and irises

The freestanding irises are made of needlelace, and
the patterns for these are provided on page 70. The
templates for the leaves are on page 75. You can make
as many flowers as you wish, though we found four
worked well. The leaves are made from green-painted
silk organza, outlined in machine stitch, though back
stitching by hand would work just as well.

You will need about twelve rocks altogether. Make
them from pieces of pressed-paper egg box, following
the method described on page 44.

Rocks

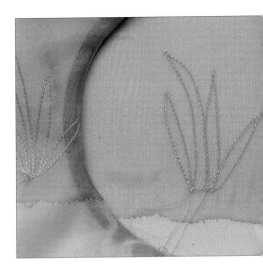

Attach four rocks at the side of the pond using stab stitch. Insert
some ferns (see page 42) into the crevices, as on page 44.

Iris leaves

Begin by painting a piece of silk
organza measuring 610 x 305mm
(24 x 12in) using green fabric
paint. Allow the silk to dry.

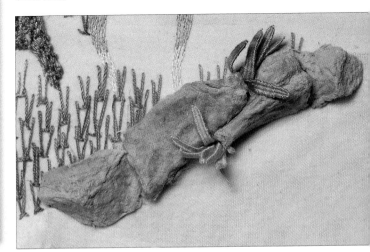

1. Fold the green-painted organza in
   half to make a piece 610 x 150mm
   (24 x 6in) and place one side of it in a
   255mm (10in) hoop. Leave enough
   spare fabric to make two more sets of
   leaves. Transfer the design using one
   of the templates provided and sew
   around the outline in green sewing
   cotton using either machine stitching
   or back stitching. Repeat this twice
   more, making three sets of double-
   thickness leaves.

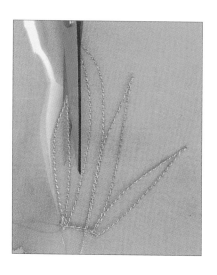

2. Take the fabric out of the hoop and cut around the leaf outlines using a pair of sharp scissors. Cut as close to the stitching as possible.

3. Attach one set of iris leaves to the embroidery, just below the base of the tree. Stab stitch along the base of the leaves only.

Iris flowers

The filling stitch for the iris petals is corded single Brussels stitch. A fine wire is incorporated into the cordonnets leaving 50mm (2in) tails, and each petal is top stitched around the edge (see page 25). There are three different types of petal, and you will need to make three of each for each flower. All the petals for each flower can be made on the same needlelace pad. Use a single strand of 100/3 fine silk and a ballpoint needle. The centres of the large petals have been worked with a deeper, orange silk thread. Full instructions on changing to a different-coloured thread are given on the facing page.

The edges of the middle-sized petals are decorated with four ring picots. Instructions for these are provided opposite.

Ring picots

Working from the left, top stitch around the edge of the shape to A. Take the needle and thread under the buttonhole stitch at B to form a loop. Make another loop back to A, and a third back to B. You now have three threads in the loop. Buttonhole over these three threads until you get back to A. Continue top stitching to C and repeat.

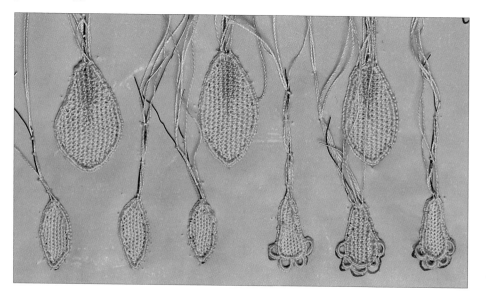

The completed petals for one of the irises, before releasing them from the needlelace pad. We made four irises altogether.

60

Changing thread colour

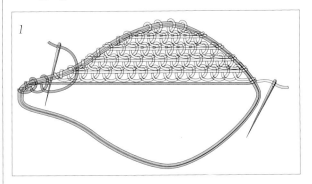

1. Work the yellow filling stitches down to the point where you want to change colour. Take the thread twice around the cordonnet. Leave the thread on the needle. Pass the orange thread through a second needle, and join it to the cordonnet on the right-hand side. Lay the thread across the shape and loop it twice around the cordonnet on the other side. Work as many orange stitches as you need into the previous row, picking up the orange cord.

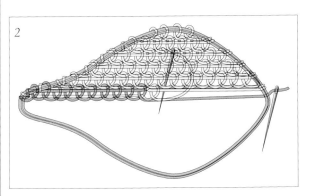

2. When you have made enough orange stitches, lay the thread across the row and under the cordonnet. Leave the needle on the thread. Pick up the needle with the yellow thread and lay the thread across the shape, taking it behind the orange stitches. Wrap the thread twice around the cordonnet on the left-hand side and bring it to the front through the last orange stitch worked. Work yellow stitches to the end of the row, picking up the yellow cord only.

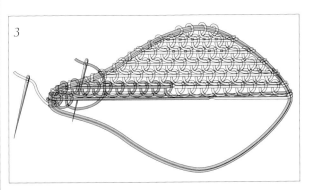

3. Take both needles under and over the cordonnet, lay both threads back across the shape and secure. In the next row, work as many stitches as you need with the orange thread over the orange cord.

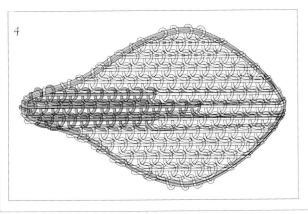

4. Pick up the yellow thread and continue across the shape working over the yellow cord. Take both needles under and over the cordonnet, lay both threads back across the shape and secure. In the next row, work as many orange stitches as you need over the orange cord. Pick up the needle with the yellow thread, bring it to the front, going through the last stitch worked, and continue across the shape. Work over the yellow cord. Finish off the orange cord by running it under some of the couching stitches on the right-hand side. Continue filling the shape with the yellow thread.

5. Bind together the three inner (smallest) petals with their top sides facing outwards. Use a single strand of green six-stranded cotton wrapped around the tops of the stems, just below the petals.

6. Using the same thread, bind in the middle-sized petals.

7. Bind in the outer petals, taking the green thread 30mm (1¼in) down the stem. Using tweezers, bend the outer and middle petals downwards, then turn the middle petals upwards at their tips.

8. Lay two irises over the first set of leaves and oversew them in place at the bases of their stems. Attach another set of leaves over the top, then the remaining two irises, and finally the third set of leaves.

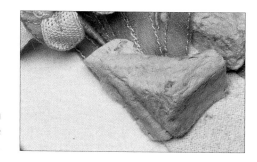

9. Attach one or two of the rocks you made earlier (see page 59) around the base of the irises.

Heron

The heron is made of gloving leather, with three layers of felt padding underneath. The templates are provided on page 76. The wing is made of needlelace, the pattern for which is given on page 72, together with detailed instructions on how to make the cordonnet on page 73.

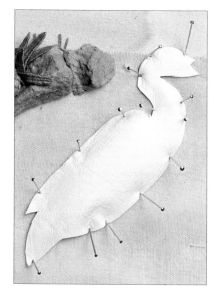

1. Attach the three layers of padding, following the instructions on page 34.

2. Cut out the shape for the heron's body from white gloving leather and pin it in place over the padding. Position the pins at the edge of the leather, where there will eventually be stitches.

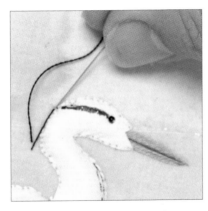

Tip

Always pin the elements in place first to ensure they are positioned correctly before stitching them.

3. Use small, neat stab stitches to secure the heron's body using white silk thread. Place stitches in the holes left by the pins so that the holes do not show. For the beak, make six long satin stitches with a single strand of orange six-stranded cotton, and one long stitch in black cotton. Attach a single black petite bead using black thread for the eye. The black markings down the front of the heron's body and on its head are drawn on using acrylic paint and a fine paintbrush.

4. Add two straight stitches, using a single strand of black cotton, to make the long, black plume on the back of the heron's head.

5. For the heron's leg, cut a 100mm (4in) length of paper-covered wire and fold it in half. Using the fine paintbrush, apply a small amount of PVA glue to one end to secure the thread, then tightly wrap the wire with pale green six-stranded cotton; leave the last 10mm (½in) bare. Wind some white cotton thread around the top of the leg. Knot each thread to finish, and cut them off leaving a long tail.

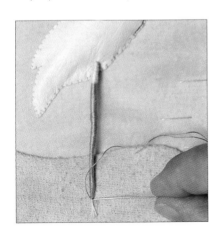

6. Lay the top of the leg over the heron's body and use the tail threads to attach the leg at the top and bottom with two or three securing stitches (the bottom of the leg will eventually be hidden under a rock).

7. Make the needlelace wing using 100/3 fine silk thread in black and grey, and a ballpoint needle. The filling stitch is corded single Brussels stitch. Follow the instructions on page 73 for the cordonnet. Attach it to the heron, using the tail threads, with two or three holding stitches spaced evenly along the top edge.

8. Place some more rocks and a fern (see page 44) around the base of the heron to cover up the bottom of the leg.

Swan

Like the heron, the swan has three layers of padding, for which templates are provided on page 76. The swan's body, however, is made of needlelace. The filling stitch used is corded single Brussels stitch, worked with two needles. The wing feathers are made as a single piece of needlelace, using the same filling stitch and worked in the same thread as the body. A thin wire is incorporated into the cordonnet to allow the wing to stand proud of the body, and top stitching applied to define the feathers. The needlelace patterns are provided on page 71, along with instructions for making the cordonnets.

1. Cut out the three layers of padding for the swan and attach them following the method described on page 34.

2. Make the swan's body using white, 100/3 fine silk thread and two No. 9 ballpoint needles. Instructions for working with two needles are provided below. Pin the needlelace in place over the padding, then secure it with stab stitches worked evenly around the outside. Attach a black petite bead using a single black cotton thread for the eye.

Making the swan's body, using two needles

Attach a white thread at A (see above) and work a foundation row of buttonhole stitches along the bottom edge and up the neck to B. Lay the thread back to A and take it under the cordonnet, but do not secure it. Leave the thread on the needle. Attach a second thread to the cordonnet and work into the loops of the preceding row, picking up the loose cord thread (see Diagram 1 opposite).

Work to the end of the row. Lay the thread back across the row, and take it under the cordonnet but do not secure it. Pick up the first needle, carefully adjust the thread tension, take it round the cordonnet once and work the row in the same way as the previous one (see Diagram 2).

Continue working with the two needles until you reach the cordonnet at C. The neck should now be complete, leaving just the swan's back to be filled. Complete the swan's body using a single needle and thread.

Make the beak, and the black marking behind the beak, using single strands of orange and black silk thread respectively. Use corded single Brussels stitch, as for the body.

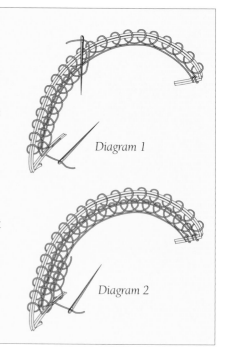

Diagram 1

Diagram 2

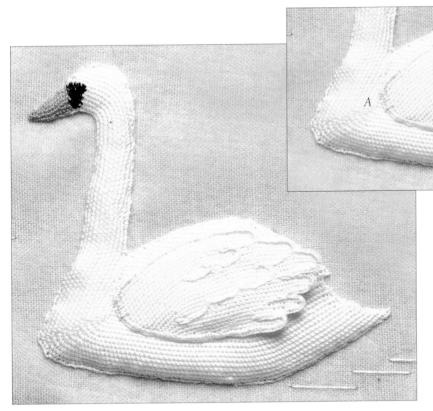

3. Make the wing using the same filling stitch as the body, and working in the same thread. Incorporate a thin wire into the cordonnet, and apply top stitching around the outside of the wing and along the edges of the feathers. Pin the wing in place, and attach it by stitching around the base, from A to B.

The completed swan.

Wader

The wader is made in the same way as the heron. Begin by attaching two layers of felt padding (see page 34), then the body, which is cut from soft gloving leather. Templates for all these shapes can be found on page 75.

The legs are paper-covered wire wrapped in a single strand of orange six-stranded cotton. Bend them into shape, and attach them in the same way as the heron's leg on page 63. Once in place, stitch on three small straight stitches at the end of each leg for feet. For the beak, make four long satin stitches with a single strand of black six-stranded cotton, and for the eye sew a single French knot using the same black thread.

Make a needlelace wing using the pattern supplied on page 70. The filling stitch is corded single Brussels stitch, worked using one strand of black 100/3 fine silk and a ballpoint needle. Apply top stitching around the cordonnet, incorporating a fine copper wire as you do so to strengthen the edge of the wing. Sew the wing to the wader's body by stab stitching along the top edge.

Fish

The fish is a piece of needlelace and is simple to make. The pattern is provided on page 72, along with instructions on how to construct the cordonnet. It is worked in corded single Brussels stitch using a single strand of variegated light blue six-stranded cotton and a ballpoint needle. The fish is attached to the background over a single layer of padding, with the lower half of its body under the blue-painted chiffon, suggesting it is jumping out of the water.

1. Make the needlelace fish. Sew a silver petite bead on to the head for an eye using one strand of blue six-stranded cotton. The two bottom fins are needle-woven picots. Follow the instructions on page 18, attaching the base of each picot (at points A, B and C) to the cordonnet by passing the needle and thread through the couching stitches. Top stitch the tail and top fin, incorporating a thin copper wire underneath the top stitching on the fin. Leave two tails of wire, approximately 25mm (1in) long.

2. Make a small, horizontal slit in the chiffon, along the gold line drawn on to the background fabric. Cut out the felt padding, slide it halfway under the chiffon and stab stitch the top part in place.

3. Position the needlelace fish over the padding, with the lower half of the fish under the chiffon, and stab stitch the upper half in place.

Frog

The needlelace frog is made in three parts – the body, the front leg and the back leg. The patterns and instructions for the cordonnet are provided on page 72. Use corded single Brussels stitch worked with one strand of variegated brown six-stranded cotton. The frog's toes have no filling stitches between the cordonnet threads; when attached to the background fabric, sew the three loops in position to look like toes.

Begin by sewing the two layers of felt padding on to the background fabric – the double layer under the frog's head serves to bring it level with the raised area of grass.

1. Attach the needlelace for the frog's body over the padding, adding small French knots for the spots, worked using a single strand of dark brown six-stranded cotton and a No. 7 embroidery needle, and a tiny black seed bead for the eye. Cut a small sliver of felt slightly smaller than the frog's front leg, and attach it to the frog's body, then sew the front leg over the padding.

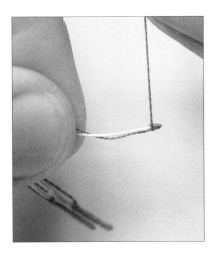

3. Bind the three lengths of wire together loosely with surgical tape to create the frog's back leg. Taper the leg from the upper part to the ankle.

2. To make the frog's back foot, cut three lengths of paper-covered wire, each 80mm (3¼in) long. Dip the tip of each one in PVA glue and wrap the first 10mm (½in) with a single strand of dark brown six-stranded cotton.

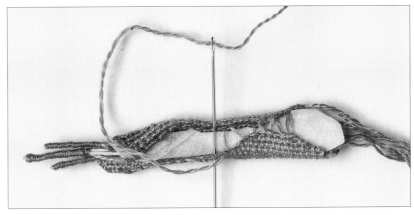

4. Wrap the needlelace around the leg, and lace the two edges together on the back using one strand of variegated brown six-stranded cotton.

5. Tuck in all the tail threads, and make two bends in the leg: one at the knee and one at the ankle.

6. Pin the back leg in place, and secure it around the upper part only, using stab stitches.

Lily and lily pads

Make the lily pads and lily using the patterns and instructions provided on page 72. Detailed instructions for the lily pads are given in the needlelace section, on page 22. Use a single strand of variegated green six-stranded cotton. The filling stitch used for the flower is corded single Brussels stitch, made using a single strand of pink six-stranded cotton. A fine wire is couched around the outside of each petal with the cordonnet threads, and then top stitching applied to give a raised edge.

The three complete lily pads. Leave long tail threads for sewing them to the background fabric.

The completed parts for the lily.

68

1. Attach each lily pad using just three or four stab stitches to hold them in place.

2. Lay on the outer background petals of the lily and secure them with two or three stab stitches around the base.

3. Secure the inner petals in the same way. Take the wires through to the back of the fabric, and bend the petals inwards towards the centre of the flower.

4. Make the stamens in the centre of the flower using turkey knot stitch (see page 19). Sew them in a row along the base of the petals. Use three strands of yellow six-stranded cotton and a No. 9 embroidery needle.

5. Attach the four larger of the individual petals in a row along the base of the flower. Twist the two end wires of each flower together first, then make a hole in the fabric with a darning needle and pass the wires through to the other side. Take the tail threads through to the back of your work and use them to overstitch the wires in place. Bend the petals outwards, away from the centre of the flower.

Tip

When arranging the petals on the background fabric, follow the numbered diagram on page 72.

6. Attach the three smaller individual petals just within the outer ones, using the same method to secure them. Bend these petals up towards the centre of the flower. Arrange all the petals to give a pleasing, three-dimensional shape to the lily.

Needlelace patterns

The following patterns are all reproduced full-size. Trace the patterns on to white paper, and use the tracings to make the needlelace pads (see page 22). The arrows on the diagrams indicate the direction of working.

Most of the cordonnets are fairly straightforward and require no explanation; for the more complicated ones, detailed instructions and a diagram are provided.

Tip

The sizes of the patterns we have provided in this book are for the needlelace we made; yours may differ in size or tension. Always check that your needlelace is the right size for your embroidery, and adjust the size or tension as necessary.

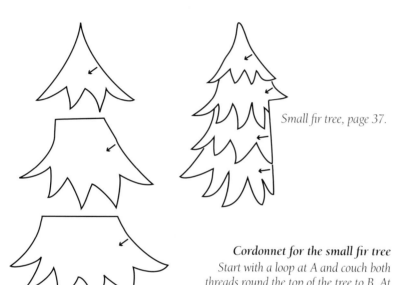

Small fir tree, page 37.

Cordonnet for the small fir tree

Start with a loop at A and couch both threads round the top of the tree to B. At B, take one thread to C, couching it down in a few places to keep it on the design line. Make a loop and couch both threads back to B. Continue couching both threads to D, then repeat the method above for D to E. Continue round to F, and repeat again for F to G. Finally couch both threads back to A and finish in the normal way.

Large fir tree, page 37.

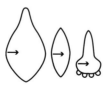

Iris petals, page 60.

Wader's wing, page 65.

Snowdrop petals, page 33.

Blossom petals,
page 46.

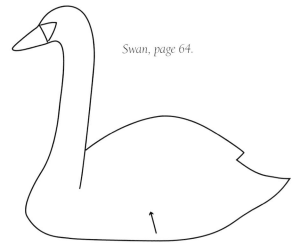

Large and small blossom leaves,
and catkin leaves, pages 46 and 48.

Cordonnet for the blossom and catkin leaves

Each leaf has a fine wire (shown in orange) incorporated into the cordonnet. Make a loop in the thread at A. Starting 25mm (1in) from the end of the wire, couch the two threads and the wire round the outside of the leaf until you get back to A. Take one of the threads and the wire up the central vein to B. Loop the thread under the couched threads, and lay it back down to A. Cut off the surplus wire, and couch down both threads and the wire back to A. Pass one thread through the loop at A, and leave two tail threads of 25mm (1in).

Swan, page 64.

Dragonfly's wings, page 33.

Cordonnet for the swan

Start with a loop at A and couch both threads round to B. Take one thread down to C and form a loop. Couch both threads back to B, pick up the thread you left behind, and continue couching both threads round to D. Take one of the threads up to E, couching it down in a few places to keep it on the design line. Make a loop around the cordonnet at E, and couch both threads back to D. Loop the thread over and under the cordonnet, and take it back to E via F, again couching it down in a few places to keep it on the design line. Make another loop at E, and couch both threads back to D via F. Pick up the other thread and couch round the rest of the shape to A. Finish in the normal way.

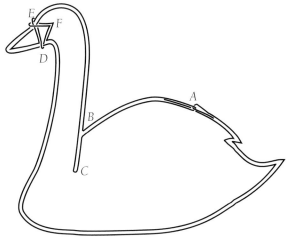

Swan's wing, page 65.

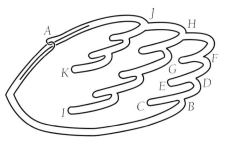

Cordonnet for the swan's wing

Start with a loop at A and couch both threads round the base of the wing to B. Take one thread to C, make a loop and couch both threads back to B. Continue round to D, and repeat for D to E, then F to G. Couch the threads round to H, then take one thread down to I, making the loops on the way back to H. Repeat for J to K. Finally couch both threads back to A and finish in the normal way.

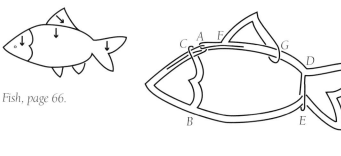

Fish, page 66.

Cordonnet for the fish

Start with a loop at A, and couch both threads round the fish's nose to B. Take one thread across to C, couching it down in a few places to keep it on the design line. At C, take the thread over and under the cordonnet and couch both threads back to B. Continue round to D, take one thread down to E, loop it round the cordonnet as before, and couch both threads back to D. Continue round to F, and take one thread back to G. Put an extra couching stitch at the tip of the fin to hold it in place. Loop the thread around the cordonnet, and couch both threads back to F. Pick up the other thread and continue to A, finishing in the normal way.

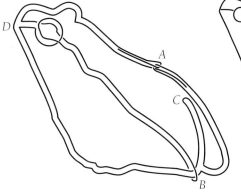

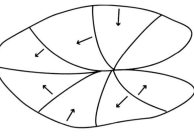

Frog's body, page 66.

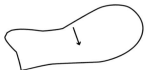

Frog's back leg, page 66.

Frog's front leg, page 66.

Cordonnet for the frog's body

Start with a loop at A and couch both threads round to B. Take one thread up to C, couching it down in a few places to keep it on the design line, make a loop, and couch both threads back to B. Continue couching round to D. Take one thread down to B, going round the eye one-and-a-half times. Loop the thread under and over the cordonnet at B and couch both threads back to D, taking the working thread round the side of the eye that has only one thread. Continue round to A and finish in the normal way.

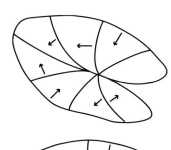

Lily pads, page 68.

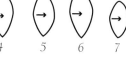

Lily petals, page 68.

Arrangement of lily petals, page 68.

Heron's wing, page 63.

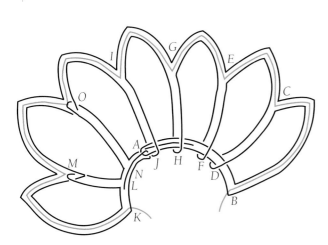

Cordonnet for the lily background petals

Start with a loop at A and couch both threads round to B. Add
a fine wire (shown in orange), and couch both threads and the
wire round to C. Leave a 25mm (1in) tail of wire. Take one
thread down to D, couching it down in a few places to keep it
on the design line, loop it under and over the cordonnet and
couch both threads back to C. Pick up the wire and the thread
you left behind, and couch both threads and the wire round to
E. Repeat the method above for E to F, G to H and I to J. From
I, couch both threads and the wire round to K. Leave the wire
at K, and couch both threads to L. Take one thread up to M,
loop it round the cordonnet and couch both threads back to L.
Take both threads to N, and repeat for N to O. From N, couch
both threads to A and finish in the normal way. Cut off the wire,
leaving a 25mm (1in) tail.

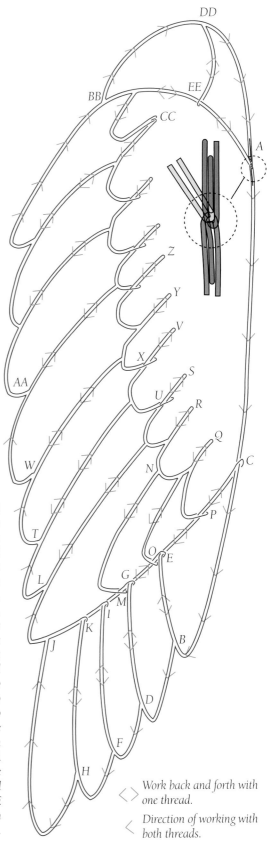

Cordonnet for the heron's wing

Cut a length of thread approximately 760mm (30in) long. Make a loop
about 200mm (7¾in) from one end and start couching at A. Couch both
threads down until you get to B. Make a branch by taking the longest thread
round to C via E, couching it down in a few places to hold it on the design
line. Loop the thread over and under the cordonnet, and couch both threads
back to B. Continue round to D, and make further branches from D to E,
F to G and H to I. From H, couch both threads to J. Take one thread to K,
loop it round the cordonnet, and couch both threads back to J. Continue
round to L. Take one thread round to M via N, couching it down on the
design line at regular intervals. At M, loop the thread round the cordonnet
and couch down both threads back to N. Repeat the process down to O, and
then to P. From P, work up to Q, put a loop in the thread and secure the loop
with a couching stitch, and continue round to R, then S, and back down to
L where you can pick up the thread you left behind. Couch both threads to
T, branch off to U, then round to V. Put in a loop at V, secured with a single
couching stitch, and couch both threads back to T. Couch round to W, then
branch off at X, Y and Z, with loops at Y and Z. Couch both threads to AA
and work the next three feathers in the same way, until you get to BB. Take
one thread to CC, loop it round the cordonnet and continue along to A and
back to BB. Continue couching both threads to DD, take one thread to EE
and back to DD, then carry on round to A to complete the cordonnet. Finish
as shown on the diagram.

⟨⟩ Work back and forth with
one thread.

⟨ Direction of working with
both threads.

73

Templates

The templates on the following pages are either full-size or half-size. The half-size templates need to be enlarged to 200 per cent to make a full-size template using a photocopier. The full-size templates can be photocopied or traced on to tracing paper.

Using the templates

For elements that need to be embroidered before being attached to the main embroidery, for example the deer and stag, make a full-size copy of the template, place it underneath the fabric, and trace around the outline using a gold gel pen. Work in a well-lit area, over a lightbox if possible.

For elements that simply need to be cut out and attached to the main embroidery, such as felt padding, and the water and grass shown below, cut out a full-size version of the template, pin it to the fabric and cut round it.

The log cabin and the fence should be photocopied and cut out, glued or simply laid on to the centre of a piece of A4 paper, and then photocopied again. The cabin and the fence are then constructed by laying the components over the equivalent parts of the template on the A4 sheet.

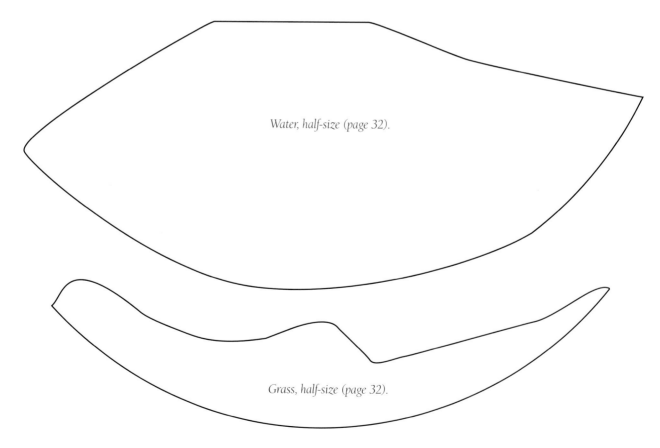

Water, half-size (page 32).

Grass, half-size (page 32).

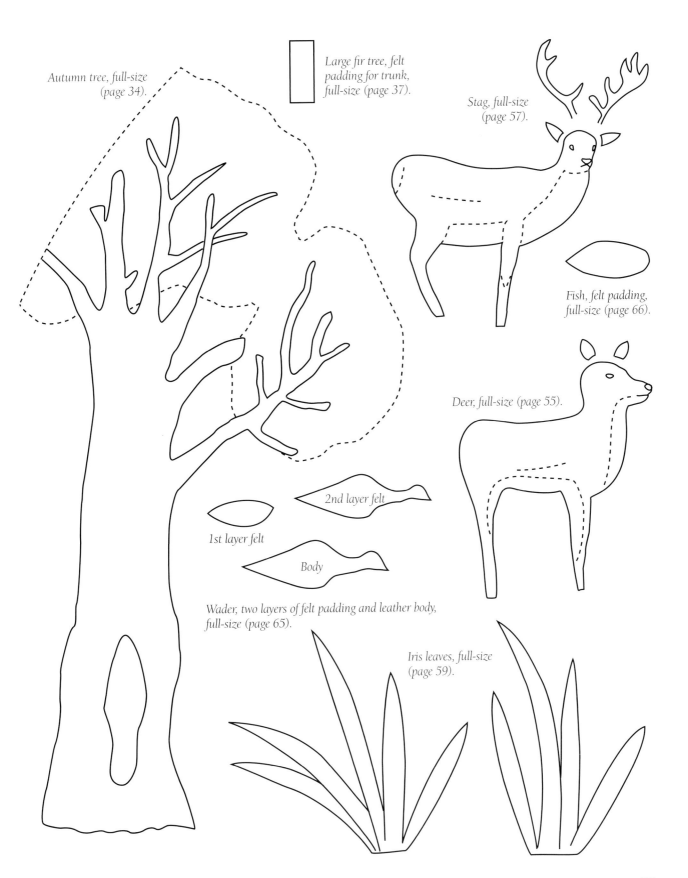

Autumn tree, full-size
(page 34).

Large fir tree, felt
padding for trunk,
full-size (page 37).

Stag, full-size
(page 57).

Fish, felt padding,
full-size (page 66).

Deer, full-size (page 55).

2nd layer felt

1st layer felt

Body

Wader, two layers of felt padding and leather body,
full-size (page 65).

Iris leaves, full-size
(page 59).

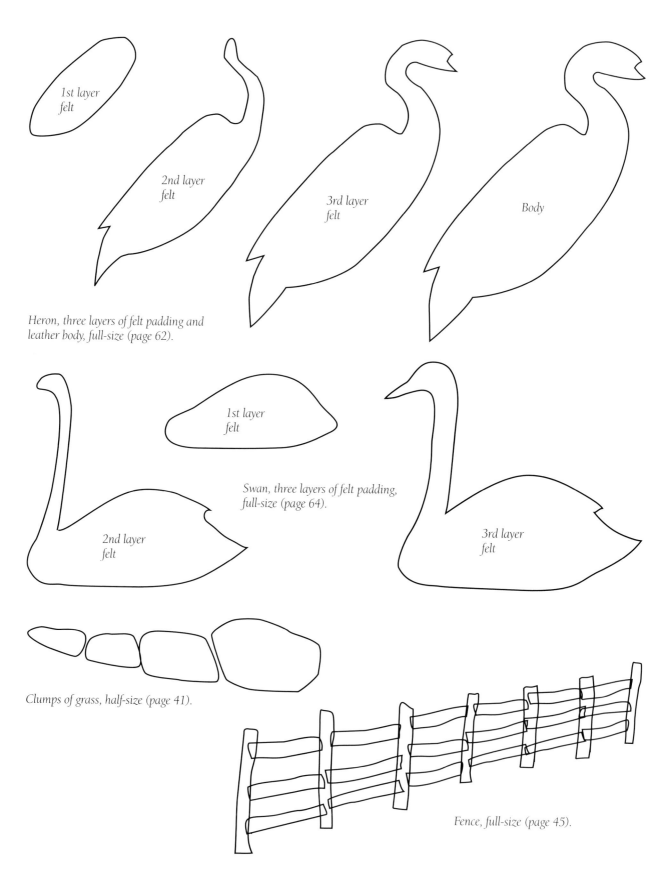

1st layer
felt

2nd layer
felt

3rd layer
felt

Body

Heron, three layers of felt padding and
leather body, full-size (page 62).

1st layer
felt

Swan, three layers of felt padding,
full-size (page 64).

2nd layer
felt

3rd layer
felt

Clumps of grass, half-size (page 41).

Fence, full-size (page 45).

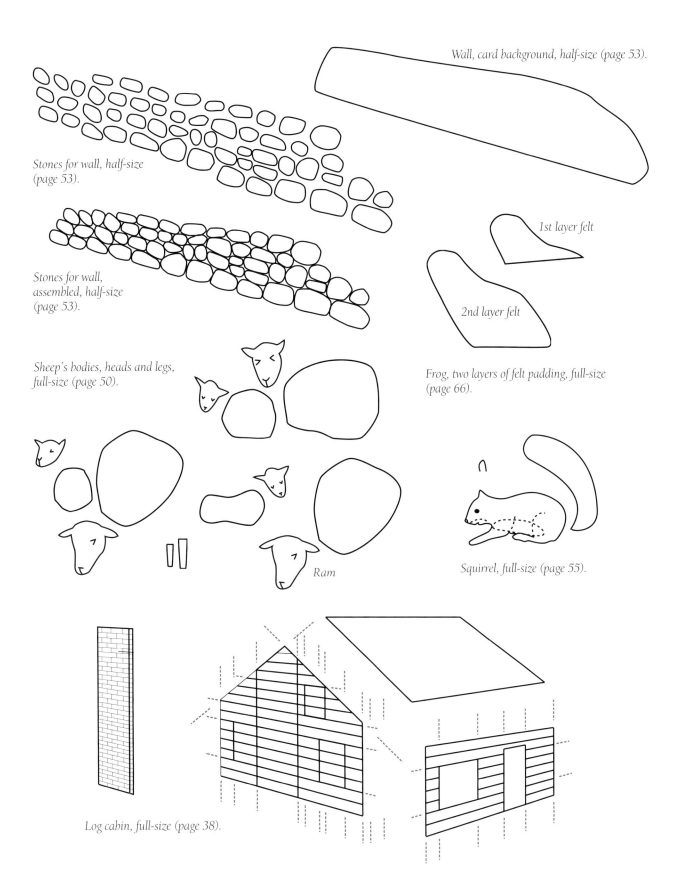

Wall, card background, half-size (page 53).

Stones for wall, half-size (page 53).

Stones for wall, assembled, half-size (page 53).

1st layer felt

2nd layer felt

Sheep's bodies, heads and legs, full-size (page 50).

Frog, two layers of felt padding, full-size (page 66).

Ram

Squirrel, full-size (page 55).

Log cabin, full-size (page 38).

Embroidery stitch diagrams

All of the embroidery stitches used in the book are shown in the following diagrams. Demonstrations of the more complicated stitches are provided on pages 14–21.

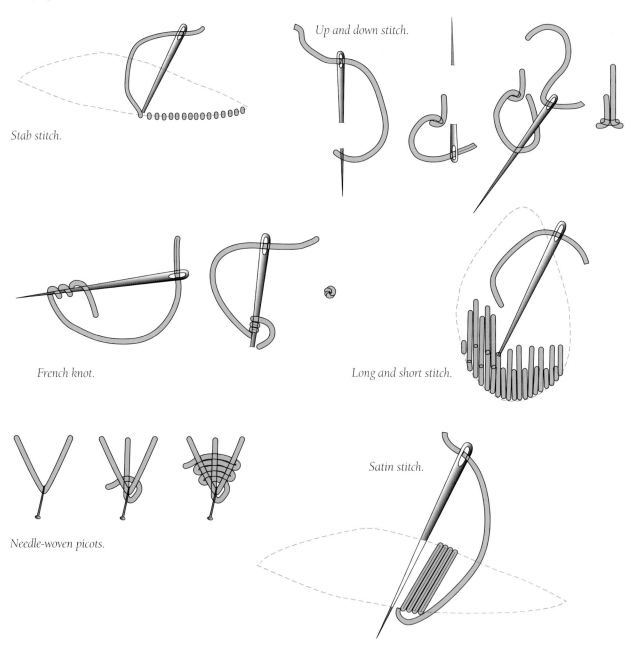

Stab stitch.

Up and down stitch.

French knot.

Long and short stitch.

Needle-woven picots.

Satin stitch.

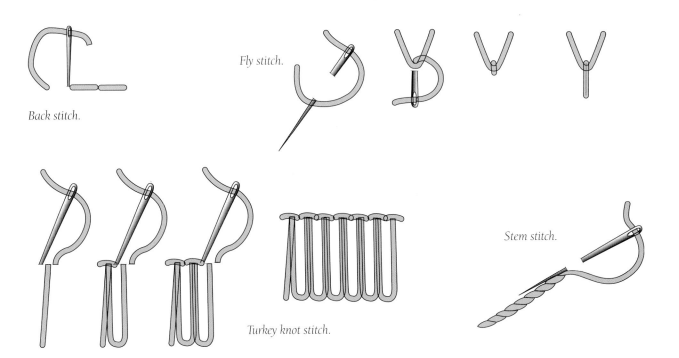

Back stitch.

Fly stitch.

Stem stitch.

Turkey knot stitch.

Padded raised chain band stitch.

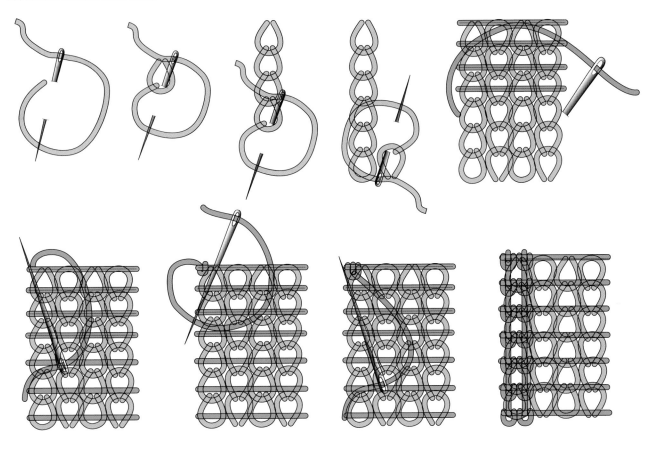

Index